SWEET BELIEVING

EIGHT CHARACTER STUDIES
OF THE
SCOTTISH COVENANTERS

By

JOCK PURVES

" Farewell, Sweet Believing."

*A Covenanter under
the sentence of death.*

STIRLING TRACT ENTERPRISE
THE DRUMMOND TRACT DEPOT
STIRLING   SCOTLAND

Sole Trade Representatives:
MARSHALL, MORGAN & SCOTT, LTD.,
33 LUDGATE HILL, LONDON, E.C.4.

Contents

Foreword

THIS book goes out into the world with very thankful remembrance of Fred, Albert, Willie and Ron, who by Red Indian axe, West African snake-bite, South American fever, and Afghan bullet laid down their lives in the preaching of the Gospel.

And also in sincere thankfulness to those dear people of the Cross, who through the years have helped in the Missionary Cause both abroad and at home. Gratitude is also due to those who have encouraged me to write.

The pages that follow are about the characters, principles and writings of the Scots Covenanters, and it is hoped that they will provide an introduction to those who would read further, fuller, and deeper about those great souls. The Covenanters are a worthy subject, and Christ is much to be admired in them.

A short bibliography is appended. It could be greatly added to.

W. E. C.,
    Livingston,
      Midlothian.

JOCK PURVES.

James Guthrie

" They have set his head on the Netherbow,
   To scorch in the summer air ;
And months go by, and the winter's snow
   Falls white on its thin grey hair.
And still that same look that in death he wore
   Is sealed on the solemn brow—
A look as of one who had travailed sore,
   But whose pangs were ended now."

Harriet Stuart Menteith.

SOME of our Zaccheus size of men, as full of faith as David, unerring in aim, have, like him, been slayers of giants. James Guthrie was one of them. He and Cromwell knew each other, and the mighty Puritan referred to him as " the short little man who could not bow." Covenanter and Puritan ! Shall we ever see their like again ? What a glorious heritage they have left to us, though somewhat now " the wild boar from the woods doth waste it."

As Joses, by the generosity of his character, won the name of Barnabas, Son of Consolation, so James Guthrie, by the stability of his character, earned the name of Sickerfoot (Sure of Foot).   And such indeed was he until he mounted the ladder to the scaffold, where he spoke for an hour, surefooted on the Rock, dying firm in his Covenanting principles.   In life and death, he fulfilled the Scripture, " stedfast, unmovable, always abounding in the work of the Lord."

One day a friend would have had him compromise a little. Said he, " Mr. Guthrie, we have an old Scots proverb, ' Jouk (duck) that the wave may gang oure ye !   Will ye nae jouk a wee bit ? ' "   And gravely Guthrie replied, " There is nae jouking in the Cause of Christ ! "   And so it was, that, unbending, surefooted, non-ducking soldier of God, he held his head high until it was taken from him, and shamefully set aloft upon a pike

5

above the thronging Netherbow Port of Edinburgh. There it bleached for twenty-seven years, till lover of the free Gospel, Sandie Hamilton, a student for the Covenanting ministry, climbed the sombre Port at the risk of his life, and, taking down the skull, buried it reverently away.

James Guthrie had much whereof he might have trusted in the flesh, amongst which was a very liberal education, given not with the object of making him a Covenanting minister. But, meeting with " yours in his Sweet Lord Jesus, Samuel Rutherford," all he had learned against the non-conforming Presbyterians vanished forever, and among them he became a preacher of the Gospel in 1638, the National Covenant signing year. His name, too, is set there on that great spiritual Magna Charta. While on his way to pen his name, he met the hangman. This moved him somewhat, and, feeling that it was prophetic, it made him walk up and down a bit before he went forward. But his signature is there in martyr lustre with the honoured names of those thousands of others on that great parchment of deerskin, " the holiest thing in all Scotland, a vow registered in Heaven." Two months before he died, he boldly confessed to the Parliament, " I am not ashamed to give God the glory that until 1638 I was treading other steps."

The last twelve years of his life were spent in Stirling, the grey fortress town whose castled rock is ever a symbol of him. Here he disciple-like lived and devotedly wrought for Christ and His Kirk. Steady in temper, he believed in the loosening up of the knots of any argument before engaging in further reasoning. Fervent in spirit, and not slothful in business, he was careful, loving and true. An undaunted fighter in a worth-while cause, and a hater of everything beneath true godliness, such as he was soon, and always, in conflict with loose living King Charles Stuart, and his like Committees. Utterly he refused such a profane ruler any authority in the affairs of the

Church. Although dismissed after one big trial, his refusal to allow the king any power over the conscience of a Christian was made much of against him in his last trials, ten years later.

He helped much to write the searching pamphlet, " The Causes of the Lord's Wrath against Scotland," and this paper was the principal pretext for his condemnation and execution. It had the honour of being put on a par with " Lex Rex " by Samuel Rutherford, and copies of both books were publicly burned by the common hangman. To hold a copy of either work was treason to King and Government. The purpose of these writings was said to be " to corrupt the minds of his majesty's loyal subjects, to alienate and withdraw them from that duty of love and obedience that they owe unto his sacred person and greatness, stirring them up against his majesty and kingly government, and containing many things injurious to the king's majesty's person and authority." But, above all that base slander, the principles they taught are those upon which the true British Constitution is based. It was a noxious doctrine that Erastus taught when he averred that a king was sovereign and supreme in all matters temporal and spiritual, and that if a church exercised powers of government and discipline in her own lawful sphere, it broke in on the authority of the magistrate. Every page of the proscribed books is for The Crown Rights of the Redeemer in His Church, the freedom of the conscience, and against the so-called Divine Right of Kings.

The wordy indictment set forth against James Guthrie gives some vivid idea of his amazing activity. " He did contrive, complot, counsel, consult, draw up, frame, invent, spread abroad or disperse,—speak, preach, declaim or utter,—divers and sundry vile seditions and treasonable remonstrances, declarations, petitions, instructions, letters, speeches, preachings, declamation and other expressions tending to the vilifying and contemning, slander and reproach of His Majesty, his progenitors, his person, majesty, dignity, authority, prerogative royal, and government."

Shortly after the Restoration of Charles II, in 1660, Guthrie, with others, was apprehended and cast into prison. In February of 1661, he was tried, and in April of that year he made a defence before the well-named Drunken Parliament. It concludes with these words, " My Lord, my conscience I cannot submit. But this old body and mortal flesh I do submit, to do with it whatsoever ye will, whether by death, or banishment or imprisonment or anything else ; only I beseech you to ponder well what profit there is in my blood. It is not the extinguishing of me or of many others that will extinguish the Covenant or work of the Reformation since 1638. My blood, bondage or banishment will contribute more for the propagation of these things than my life in liberty would do, though I should live many years." At the close of this speech, some members withdrew, saying that they would have no part in his death, and one made a strong appeal urging banishment. But his judges were baying for his blood, and he, with Captain William Govan, a fit companion, was sentenced to be hanged at Edinburgh Cross on June 1st, 1661. The head of Guthrie was to be stuck upon a pike high above the Netherbow Port, his estate confiscated, and his family arms torn. The head of Govan, pike-stuck, was likewise to be high up on the West Port. On receiving this sentence, Guthrie said to the members of the Drunken Parliament, " My Lords, let never this sentence affect you more than it does me, and let never my blood be required from the King's family." But it was required, with the blood of many others, in the fulness of time.

While lying in the Tolbooth, he saw Archibald Campbell, Marquis of Argyle, " not afraid," as Argyle said, " to be surprized by fear," going forth with Highland Christian dignity to his martyrdom. Said Guthrie, " Such is my respect for your Lordship that were I not under sentence of death myself I could cheerfully die for your Lordship." There was but a week between their meeting and their parting. He told his wife, " I am more fortunate than the Great Marquis, for my Lord was beheaded, but I am to be hanged on a tree as my Saviour was." She wept sorely when for the last time she parted from him. " I do but trouble you," she said. " I must now part from you." And he replied, " Henceforth I know no man after the flesh."

James Cowie, his dear friend manservant, was with him in the Tolbooth, and he tells us that James Guthrie ever kept through his busy life his own personal fellowship with Christ, in the fresh joyous bloom of his new birth, as if he had been but a young convert ; and thus it wondrously was till his last earth day dawned, and the summer sun streamed in through the iron bars of his cell windows. Sure-of-Foot arose at about four o'clock for worship, and was asked by Cowie how he was. " Very well," said Guthrie. " This is the day that the Lord hath made ; let us rejoice and be glad in it." Soon was to be fulfilled the prophecy of his godly cousin, William Guthrie, of Fenwick, author of the spiritual classic, " The Christian's Great Interest." He had said, " Ye will have the advantage of me, James, for ye will die honourably before many witnesses with a rope about your neck, and I shall die whinging upon a wee pickle straw." This was the day, and the Lord had made it, and his confessed desire, called by him a lust, was to be granted, that he should die for his Saviour.

His two little children, Sophia and William, came to see him. Taking five-year-old William on his knee, he said to him, " Willie, the day will come when they will cast up to you that your father was hanged. But be not thou ashamed, lad. It is in a good cause." Little Sophia and her mother were banished from the country, and part of the savage sentence was that the children and their posterity should be beggars forever—which was not to reckon with Him who takes beggars from the dunghill and sets them among princes, and Who will not see the righteous forsaken nor his seed begging bread. On that fatal afternoon of the day of his father's death, while children more knowing were running at the sound of the drum's frightening tattoo, it was with difficulty that wee Willie Guthrie was restrained, by James Cowie, from playing in the streets.

With hands tied together, James Guthrie walked slowly up the High Street to the city cross. Broad-shouldered William Govan kept pace beside him. The one nearly fifty, the other not yet out of his thirties, Greatheart and Valiant for Truth were once more upon the human scene. Soon they were upon the scaffold above the serried rows of glittering steel, and Sicker-foot, who had been offered a bishopric, and had refused it, stepped forward with loving zeal to give his last message. The great crowd stood hushed to hear him say, " I take God to record upon my soul, I would not exchange this scaffold with the palace and mitre of the greatest prelate in Britain. Blessed be God who has shown mercy to me such a wretch, and has revealed His Son in me, and made me a minister of the Ever-lasting Gospel, and that He hath deigned, in the midst of much contradiction from Satan, and the world, to seal my ministry upon the hearts of not a few of His people, and especially in the station where I was last, I mean the congregation and presbytery of Stirling. Jesus Christ is my Life and my Light, my Righteousness, my Strength, and my Salvation and all my desire. Him ! O Him, I do with all the strength of my soul commend to you. Bless Him, O my soul, from henceforth even forever. Lord, now lettest Thou Thy servant depart in peace for mine eyes have seen Thy salvation." A copy of his last testimony was handed by him to a friend, for his son William when he should come to years. Then farther up the ladder of death he went, exclaiming, " Art not Thou from everlasting, O Lord my God. I shall not die but live." And in his last second before he was with Christ, Mr. Sickerfoot, as sure of foot, and as full of faith as Joshua, lifted the napkin from his face, crying, " The Covenants ! The Covenants ! They shall yet be Scotland's reviving."

Captain William Govan, intently watching, stood by. His martial shoulders were squared. Gazing lovingly at the dangling dead minister of Christ he thought of Calvary's Tree. " It is sweet ! It is sweet ! " he cried, " otherwise how durst I look with courage upon the corpse of him who hangs there, and smile upon these sticks and that gibbet as the very Gates of Heaven." The hangman had him prepared. The brave soldier taking a ring from a finger, gave it to a friend, asking him to carry it to his wife, and to tell her that he died in humble confidence and found the Cross of Christ sweet, and that Christ had done all for him, and that it was by Him alone that he was justified. Someone called to him to look up to the Lord Jesus, and he smilingly said, " He looks down and smiles at me." Ascending the ladder, these words from him rang out across the crowds, " Dear friends, pledge this cup of suffering as I have done, before you sin, for sin and suffering have been presented to me and I have chosen the suffering part." The rope adjusted he ended his witness with, " Praise and glory be to Christ forever." A little pause, a little prayer, the signal given, and all was over and he too swung in the fresh summer air. Another who had magnified Christ in life, had magnified Him also in death.

Later, friends came for the bodies from which the heads had been removed. They were lovingly laid out and arranged for burial, while the heads were put up in grisly fashion above the Netherbow and West Ports.

Day by day, week by week, little feet pattered over the cobbles to the Netherbow, and young pained wondering eyes looked up at the head high above them, and returning to what home he had, little Willie Guthrie would hide himself away for hours, saying, when found, " I've seen my faither's heid ! I've seen my faither's heid ! " In childhood, boyhood and youth, in summer suns and winter storms, he saw the head that was given for Christ, " my faither's heid ! " He, too, was for Christ Jesus and the Covenants, spending much time alone in prayer " a serious seeker after God." He became a scholar of excellent promise, and bent his steps after his father to a suffering ministry. But he sickened, and died, and his young head was laid in the earth while the bleached skull of his father still witnessed high above the Netherbow Port of Edinburgh.

*   *   *   *

William Guthrie of Fenwick endeavoured to go to the execution of his valued cousin, but he was prevented from doing so by fellow-believers. They feared for his life. This truly wonderful man of God, banished from his church, died a few years later " whinging (groaning) on his wee pickle straw " (died in his bed). He had a complication of diseases, and passed away in great agonies, but was uncomplaining in his suffering. He said, " The Lord has been kind to me, notwithstanding all the evils I have done, and, I am assured, that though I should die mad, I shall die in the Lord. Blessed are the dead that die in the Lord at all times ; but more especially when a flood of errors, snares, and judgments are beginning or coming on a nation, church or people." A student under Samuel Ruther-ford, he received through him his call to the ministry in some-thing of the fear and terror of the Lord. This turned to a joy and peace in believing which thrilled and filled him to the end. Only forty-five when he died, he was accounted, in Scotland, the greatest preacher of his day. He was the means of bringing thousands to Christ, and of establishing thousands in Christ. His lasting monument is his book, " The Christian's Great Interest," probably one of the most spiritual books ever written. On this we have the word of John Owen, " and, for a divine (taking out of his pocket a small gilt copy of Guthrie's treatise) that author I take to be one of the greatest divines that ever wrote. It is my vade mecum ; I carry it and the Sedan New Testament still about me. I have written several folios, but there is more divinity in it than in them all." The famous Welsh-English Puritan, in lowliness of mind, was esteeming another better than himself. But what a commendation, to get such a word from John Owen, " A scribe everyway instructed in the mysteries of the Kingdom of God, in conversation he held up to many, in his public discourses to more, in his publications from the press to all, who were set out for the Celestial Zion, the effulgent lamp of evangelical truth to guide their steps to immortal glory."

B

Hugh Mackail

" Sing with me, sing with me, sing with me !
 Blessed spirits sing with me ;
 To the Lamb our song shall be
 Through a glad eternity.

" Farewell earthly morn and even,
 Sun and moon and stars of heaven.
 Heavenly portals ope before me ;
 Sing with me, sing with me, sing with me,
 Blessed spirits sing with me."

JAMES HOGG (Covenanters' Scaffold Song).

AS a boy, when winter winds were howling, and the rains were pouring down, I used to sometimes shiver, thinking of Covenanters, a godly nine hundred of them, in the bleak winter of 1666, straggling through my boyhood town, journeying on to the Pentland Hills and tragic Rullion Green. Some of them were tied hand to hand so that the stronger among them might urge on the weaker. In pitiless weather, they reached the hills and " cold-footed and wet-shod " stayed the night.

In all seasons, the Pentland Hills are beautiful to see. But they carry Nature's bounty of beauty crowned, for many of the Redeemed of the Lord lie among them. In literature, the famous name linked with them is that of Robert Louis Stevenson who lived beside them. They were his own " hills of home." He studied much the literature of the Covenant, even to saying in one of his letters from far-away Samoa that his wondrous style was fashioned by Covenanter writers. " I have been accustomed," he writes, " to hear refined and intelligent critics —those who know so much better what we are than we do ourselves—trace down my literary descent from all sorts of people, including Addison, of whom I could never read a word. Well, low in your ear, sir, the clue was found ! My style is from the Covenanting writers." And he never forgot, and wrote, " A Cry from Samoa."

> " Blows the wind to-day, and the sun and the rain are flying,
> Blows the wind on the moors to-day, and now
> Where about the graves of the martyrs the whaups are crying
> My heart remembers how.
>
> Grey recumbent tombs of the dead in desert places,
> Standing stones on the vacant wine-red moor,
> Hills of sheep, and the homes of the silent vanished races,
> And winds austere and pure.
>
> Be it granted me to behold you again in dying,
> Hills of home, and to hear again the call,
> Hear about the graves of the martyrs the pewits crying,
> And hear no more at all."

At Rullion Green, among the hills, eight thousand well-fed, well-armed dragoons and guards reached the haggard and homeless nine hundred, who formed up, having chosen " never to break until He who had brought them together should break them." Prayer was made and verses were sung from the 71st and 78th Psalms, and they strengthened one another's hands in the Lord, waiting for the onset, prepared to live Christ, or to greatly gain in death. They were of the school who know the permitted power of the devil, and in adversity rebel not against God, but bless the Name of the Lord, as Job of old, neither sinning nor charging God foolishly. They believed that their sufferings were as blood-washed as their sins. " Brother, die well, it is the last act of faith you will ever be able to do," was the advice of one Covenanter to another, sick and dying. Their Master kept His good and best wine to the last on dark Mount Calvary, and in bringing many sons into glory He brings them this way too ; and thus it was on wintry Rullion Green, the good and best wine at the last.

Once in the morning, and twice in the afternoon, these

wearied countrymen beat off heavy attacks ; but multitudes told and the massacre began of the almost unarmed men of His Blood, King Jesus, by the eight to one " belligods " of the man of blood, King Charles. In a few terrible hours, was come to pass again the Scriptures, " For Thy sake we are killed all the day long ; we are accounted as sheep for the slaughter," and, thanks be to God, " nay, in all these things we are more than conquerors through Him that loved us." Darkness fell on dead and wounded Psalm Singers lying all around, the reddened blades descending on others, and more escaping to be as the rabbit or the fox upon the hunting field. Here and there were groups of unkempt, half-naked prisoners who were to be kept as beasts for the shambles, in freezing winter day and night till " the Grassmarket heard them preach from the red scaffold floor." But whether it be on stricken field, in torture, on scaffold, or in banishment, there is no record of any who had been at Pentland ever going back from their Lord, or abjuring their Covenant made with Him. To read their testimonies is a spiritual experience never to be forgotten. They were executed in ones, twos, threes, fours, and even ten at a time. Their heads, and right hands, in some cases, were sent to be put up in towns as gruesome warnings. But listen to them if you would know something of the Scripture, " He shall see of the travail of His soul, and shall be satisfied." Here is the merchant, John Wodrow, on his dying day writing to his wife, " O, my heart, come and see, I beseech you ! I thought that I had known something of my dearest Lord before. But never was it so with me as since I came within the walls of this prison. He is without all comparison ! O love, love Him ! O taste and see ! And that shall solve the question best."

The soldier, Andrew Arnot, speaks from his last field of fight, " I do account myself highly honoured to be reckoned among the witnesses of Jesus Christ, to suffer for His Name,

Truth and Cause ; and this day I esteem it my glory, garland, crown and royal dignity to fill up a part of His sufferings." The country landlord, John Neilson, heart free from his possessions, cries, " If I had many worlds I would lay them all down, as now I do my life for Christ and His Cause." They were exultant in their pure fervent love of the Master. Another voice spoke raucously clear in their times, that of the vile raging vices of their persecutors.

It is in the ordering of the Most High that so much has been bequeathed to us of credible writing by and for the Covenanters. And as regards the martyrs of Pentland, the fine old volume, " Naphtali, my Wrestling," is invaluable. It was published first in 1667, the year following Pentland Fight. It is no " Mein Kampf," the struggle of a Hitler, but something so different. It is Naphtali, real wrestlings of the Church of God for the Kingdom of God. In it is testimony after testimony of " grace upon grace," and " from glory to glory."

It is noteworthy that about seventeen years after Rullion Green, " The Children's Bond " should be drawn up and signed by fifteen young girls in the village of Pentland. One of these girls, Beatrice Umpherston, was only ten years of age. It is evident that firesides in Pentland held much of conversation about Christ and His claims that the merry minds of the young were spiritually impressed, and stilled to sober covenanting with Him. Part of the Bond reads, " This is a Covenant between the Lord and us, to give up ourselves fully to Him, without reserve, soul and body, hearts and affections, to be His children and Him to be our God and Father, if it please the Holy Lord to send His Gospel to the land again." And then there is their prayer, " O Lord, give us real grace in our hearts to mind Zion's breaches, that is in such a low case this day, and make us to mourn with her, for Thou hast said, them that mourn with her in the time of her trouble shall rejoice when she rejoiceth." No doubt, there were older alert holy minds and devout hearts behind all this, suffering little children to come unto Him, but how heart-warming it all is, that in a mad day when men were murderously hated for reasonably loving Him, out of the mouths of some children was perfected praise.

*   *   *   *

One of the prisoners of Pentland who through physical weakness had not been able to be with his friends at the time of battle, was Hugh MacKail, a scholarly young minister of twenty-five years of age. Richly gifted and very spiritual, the excellency of the power of God apparent in him, he had his treasure in an earthen vessel already breaking from a destroying consumption. He had been licensed to preach at twenty, and preached his last public sermon at twenty-one in the Kirk of St. Giles, Jenny Geddes' battle-ground. There were words in that sermon some could never forget. " The fountain," said MacKail, " whence violence flows may be great power which the Church cannot reach. The Scripture doth abundantly evidence that the People of God have been persecuted sometimes by a Pharaoh on the throne, sometimes by a Haman in the State, and sometimes by a Judas in the Church." There was no need of further roll-call. Pharaoh, Haman, and Judas answered to their names, and he had to go into hiding from that very day. Holland was a haven to many a Covenanter, as it was to many a Puritan, and Hugh MacKail landed safely there to become more fitted to return to the unsafe land, the Bloody Land of Scotland. In 1666, he was back again ready to be offered as that cruel year closed. A hectic flush was on his cheeks, but in the mists and rains with the wanderers was also valiant Hugh MacKail. So that though not able to be in the Rullion Green fight, he was not far away, and easily taken. In due course, he appeared before a Council who seemed to think that he would tell them much. But he quietly refused to tell them anything at all, and the violent Earl of Rothes, convulsed with passion, adjudged the dying field preacher worthy of the torture of the bone and marrow mixing Boot.

Sir Walter Scott, though no reliable judge of Covenanters or their principles, limned some of his most interesting characters from Covenanting models, and upon Covenanting canvas. It is to be regretted that he did not understand such admirable people, but his great books that in any way concern them, such as " The Heart of Mid Lothian," " Old Mortality," and " Redgauntlet," will be read by some time and again even for the Covenanters' worthy sakes. Sir Walter gives a vivid description of that cruel instrument the Boot, and of its bestial torture. " The executioner enclosed the leg and knee within the tight iron case, and then placing a wedge of the same metal between the knee and the edge of the machine, took a mallet in his hand and stood waiting for further orders. A surgeon placed himself by the other side of the prisoner's chair, bared the prisoner's arm, and applied his thumb to the pulse in order to regulate the torture according to the strength of the patient. When these preparations were made, the President glanced his eye around the Council as if to collect their sufferings, and judging from their mute signs, gave a nod to the executioner whose mallet instantly descended on the wedge, and forcing it between the knee and the iron boot, occasioned the most exquisite pain, as was evident from the flush on the brow and cheeks of the sufferer."

A thin wasted limb of weak Hugh MacKail was placed within this hell-invented instrument, and the brutal wedge was driven home eleven savage times till the leg was smashed and pulpy, but no word of betrayal or of accusation of his brethren stained the lips of the young Covenanter. Unmoved by his afflictions, he was carried down into his dungeon to lie in painful intercession for his fellows, who outside on the gallows, died in purity and piety for the sake of the Name " in the power and sweetness thereof," in the cold sea-tanged air of Edinburgh.

Again Hugh MacKail appeared before the men with the power of Pilate, and they in Pilate weakness condemned him to die at the Mercat Cross of Edinburgh. But he who lived in the power of a deeper death, and had the sentence of it in himself, was borne with shining face down to the Tolbooth through the large crowds who openly wept as he passed. " Trust in God," he called to them, " Trust in God ! " Getting a fleeting glimpse of a well-known friend, he shouted in ecstasy, " How good is the news ! Four days now until I see Jesus ! " In prison, a merry thrill of joy was on him making him humorous in serious hours. Someone asking him how his crushed leg was faring, he smilingly replied that the fear of his neck was making him forget his leg. And he averred that he was less cumbered about dying than he had often been about preaching a sermon ! His old minister father came to see him, and they strengthened and comforted each other in the love of the Father and the Son.

The night before his execution he went to rest at about eleven o'clock, and his doctor cousin, Matthew MacKail, lay by him. Doctor Matthew had gone to Archbishop Sharp for help, but " the Judas in the Church " had not forgotten, and his answer was, " I can do nothing." To this the doctor replied, " You mean, I will do nothing." Hugh was astir by five o'clock, and awoke John Wodrow, the Glasgow merchant, who, with several other Covenanters, was to die beside him. " Up, John," he said, smiling, " you and I do not look like men about to be hanged, seeing we lie so long." But, as one having no fellowship with the throne of iniquity, earnestly he prayed, " Lord, we come to Thy throne, a place we hitherto have not been acquainted with. Earthly kings' thrones have advocates against poor men, but Thy throne has Jesus Christ an Advocate for us. Our prayer this day is not to be free from death, but

that we may witness before many witnesses a good confession."
His prayer was answered abundantly, and they who were seen
in the weakness and scandal of the Cross showed forth the
Power of His Resurrection.

In 1496, Savanarola preached his famous sermon, " The
Art of Dying a Good Death." He said, " Death is the most
solemn moment of our life. Then it is that the Evil One makes
his last attack on us. It is as though he were always playing
chess with man, and awaiting the approach of death to give him
checkmate. He who wins at that moment wins the battle of
life." And Girolamo Savanarola, the Evangelical Dominican,
won his battle of life through the Power of Life Abundant
in his last dread painful day, and so also did Hugh MacKail,
Covenanter.

Up that eloquent path of his nation's history, the High
Street of Edinburgh, the godly youth struggled along to the
gallows. Crowds groaning and in tears watched him as he
passed. " He was fairer and of a more stayed countenance
than ever before," they said. Looking over the great concourse
of solemn people, joyous faith suffused him, and he cried aloud
in a rapture, " So there is a greater and more solemn preparation
in Heaven to carry my soul to Christ's Bosom."

On the scaffold, he took out his Testimony which the great
old volume, Naphtali, has preserved for us. He read it to the
vast crowds, " a singularly beautiful confession of fidelity and
devotion." He had got what he said, "a clear ray of the Majesty
of the Lord." His song of praise then lifted up into the echoes
of the old city an unashamed waiting for God, a rejoicing in
salvation. It was from the 31st Psalm :

> " Into Thine hands I do commit
> My Spirit ; for Thou art he.
> Oh, Thou, Jehovah, God of truth,
> Thou hast redeemed me."

Up the ladder to the rope he climbed, crying, " I care no more to go up this ladder, and over it, than if I were going home to my father's house." Rung by rung he called aloud, " Every step is a degree nearer Heaven." Sitting at the top of the ladder he took out his pocket Bible, and, after addressing the crowds, he read from the last chapter of it. Standing up, the napkin was put over his face, but, lifting it, in a remarkable voice by faith inspired, he burst forth into an ecstatic offering of farewells and welcomes filled with grace and glory, probably the most blessed wondrous and glorious Amen of comparisons ever uttered :

" Now, I leave off to speak any more to creatures, and turn my speech to Thee, O Lord. Now, I begin my intercourse with God which shall never be broken off. Farewell, father and mother, friends and relations ! Farewell, the world and all delights ! Farewell, meat and drink ! Farewell, sun, moon and stars ! Welcome God and Father ! Welcome Sweet Lord Jesus, Mediator of the New Covenant ! Welcome Blessed Spirit of Grace, God of all Consolation ! Welcome Glory ! Welcome Eternal Life ! Welcome Death ! " The bloody rope tightened around his thin young neck. The watching crowds groaned dismally. And then was witnessed something surely unparalleled. " Love never faileth," and the great unfailing quality, unable to do any more in life, would help in death. Dr. Matthew MacKail stood below the gallows, and as his martyr cousin writhed in the tautened ropes, he clasped the helpless jerking legs together and clung to them that death might come the easier and sooner. And so with Christ was Hugh MacKail " with his sweet boyish smile." " And that will be my welcome," he had said, " the Spirit and the Bride say, Come."

Later, the young Covenanter was laid out in the Magdalene Chapel and dressed there for burial. Not all his fellow-martyrs were allowed this. He was laid in the earth of Grey-friars Kirkyard, where the National Covenant was signed, two years before he was born. Many saw him laid away in the corner reserved for criminals, the usual bed for the Covenanter martyr from the gallows. Many had gone before and many followed. It is a much frequented sacred corner now where stands the Martyrs' Monument. The crowds go up beyond to the great and noble War Memorial high above upon the Castle Rock, but even in the snows of winter there is a well worn path to the Martyrs' grave among the wicked.

Dr. Matthew MacKail missed, till the end of his days, his godly cousin, and in his deep mourning for him, wore for as long as it could be put on, the martyr's own black haircloth coat, requested by the doctor himself from the hangman.

*   *   *   *

Pentland Martyrs ! The grand old history by Wodrow has it like this, " I hear, most, if not all of them, left their written testimonies behind them, and it is a pity any of them are lost. Scarce the half of them are in Naphtali. Though some of them lived long in bondage through fear of death, and others of them had some anguish of body through the wounds received in Pentland, their torture, and other pieces of ill treatment afterward, yet all of them died in great serenity and peaceful hope of salvation."

Richard Cameron

"Cameron of the Covenant stood
And prayed the battle prayer;
Then with his brother side by side
Took up the Cross of Christ and died
Upon the Moss of Ayr."

HENRY INGLIS (*Hackston of Rathillet*).

SANQUHAR Town, 22nd June, 1680! A band of about twenty horsemen are clattering up the High Street to the Town Cross! People are running to see them! "It's Richie," they cry, "it's Richie Cameron! Here are the Hillmen!"

It is Richard Cameron, Lion of the Covenant, a Richard Coeur-De-Lion, indeed, with some of the Faithful Remnant. He and his brother Michael dismount. The others form a circle about them. It is the first anniversary of the Bothwell Brig slaughter, and, for the murder of their comrades, this is their answer, the inestimably brave Sanquhar Declaration. In clear and solemn tones, Michael Cameron reads that they "disown Charles Stuart, who hath been reigning, or rather tyrannising, as we may say, on the throne of Britain these years bygone, as having any right, title to, or interest in, the said crown of Scotland for Government, as forfeited several years since by his perjury and breach of covenant both to God and His Kirk, and usurpation of His Crown and Royal Prerogatives therein . . . As also we being under the Standard of our Lord Jesus Christ, Captain of Salvation, do declare a war with such a tyrant and usurper, and all the men of his practices, as enemies to our Lord Jesus Christ, and His Cause and Covenants, and against all such as have strengthened him . . . As also we disown, and by this, resent the reception of the Duke of York,

24

that professed Papist, as repugnant to our Principles and Vows to the Most High God." The high born wretch, the Duke of York, had sneeringly threatened to make parts of Scotland like a hunting field. From the hunted who knew him as " The devil's lieutenant," this was the answer. Thomas Campbell nailed up the fearless words. Another prayer, a verse or two of a Psalm, and those men of forfeited lives disappeared among their welcoming hills.

Eight years later, the Lords Spiritual and Temporal, and the Commons of England with the Estates of Scotland, flung out King James Stuart, and put William and Mary upon the British Throne. It was but a following of the brave resolute few of the Sanquhar Declaration. As Carlyle has it, " how many earnest rugged Cromwells, Knoxes, Poor Peasant Covenanters wrestling, battling for very life, in rough miry places, have to struggle, and suffer, and fall, greatly censured, bemired, before a beautiful Revolution of Eighty-Eight can step over them in official pumps and silk stockings with universal three times three ! " Richard Cameron truly prophesied, " Ours is a standard which shall overthrow the Throne of Britain." It did.

* * * *

To-day, Ulster, Northern Ireland, is probably the most evangelically Christian part of Britain. This is the work of God. Had Eire, Southern Ireland, known the gracious change experienced by the rest of Britain at the Glorious Reformation, the history of our nation, religiously, socially and politically, would have been vastly different, and all for the better. But Rome still has its spreading power among us, and mostly from this one source, the noxious power that is at one with that of Spain, Portugal and South America. It does not carry the light of the Reformation, the Light of the Gospel. But Ulster is part of God's answer. And Ulster is a Covenanting triumph, and it was right that the last crushing blows against Stuart

Romanism should be struck by Covenanter and Puritan at Londonderry, Inniskilling and the Boyne. It was in Ulster that Covenanters with Puritans settled in their godly thousands, and often moved, as they termed it, " from one bloody land to another." The " No Surrender " of Derry is the echo of the Covenanter cry, " The Lord our Righteousness." And so the blessing of God to the generations has lasted through the centuries, and is there to-day. It is not political partition only that is in Ireland. It is a fundamental partition. It is that between people and people, between the open Bible and pure evangelical faith, and a power that would draw back again into a dense darkness from which there has been a merciful deliverance. But there are two great dangers in Ulster as elsewhere in this country. These are mere nominal Protestantism and Modernism. May the people so blessedly placed inherit their heritage, winning Christ.

The present compilers of the Scottish National Dictionary have not forgotten Ulster either, and say, " The Scottish National Dictionary deals with the vocabulary of literary and spoken Scots, including the dialects of the mainland, Orkney, Shetland and Ulster, from 1700 to the present day." Ulster is a British Covenanting triumph, and God's blessing still is there. May the people speaking the language of their fathers, speak it in the Grace of God, as they most clearly did.

The U.S.A. too is a great result of the further development of the Reformation in the orderings of the Most High. It might have been settled in as Spanish or Portuguese, and, therefore, now been as South America, Romish, backward and dark. But in genius and constitution, in its strong depths and on its grand heights, it is a Protestant land. This is because of a people, such a people, in moral and spiritual stature incomparable, the finest expositors of Scripture ever known, the English Puritans. The power of Scripture going before, and the power of Scripture following after, are all of one in the Cross of the Lord Jesus. Abraham and his call, and the Pilgrim Fathers sailing out, are set in Calvary. Carrying banished men and women, with their little children, the " Mayflower " was an earnest of a summer of spiritual bloom to be followed by a great harvest. The people of God suffer but to reign. Through the Cross, it was again the lines falling in pleasant places—a promise and also a fulfilment of the Love and Grace of God. And so these Blood-brothers of the Covenanters went out and founded a nation like their own—lands of free men, lands of the Gospel of the Grace of Christ from which to other races the Message of the Redeming Love of God has been taken forth unceasingly. It was King Charles Stuart that caused these people to go, but God meant it unto good. Other ships were making ready to sail, but Charles of Divine Right imperiously forbade their going. Had he but known he would have had them go, and that quickly, for two of the names of the would-be Pilgrim Colonists were Oliver Cromwell and John Hampden ! Oh those days of seeming calamity to those brave and noble hearts ! Those were days of the planting of the Lord. The British Commonwealth and the United States of America are the works of sufferers for His Name's Sake, enduring and achieving by faith.

* * * *

Alan Cameron, believing merchant in Falkland, Fife, had three sons of whom Richard was the eldest. The other two, Michael and Alexander, were also believers, and followed the Covenanting Banner of Blue. The only daughter, Marion, was a sincere Christian woman who died at the hands of violent dragoons.

After his university days, Richard Cameron was a school-master, but he knew not the Saviour. Sometimes he listened to the here-on-earth-today and there-in-heaven-tomorrow Field Preachers, and one day, obtaining mercy and finding grace, listened unto Life. His own voice was soon heard among theirs, as of a trumpet clear and certain, and thousands listened to him. He was white hot himself and had little use for the lukewarm. By his sincere example he inspired many. Even in the cold shadow of the gallows, just before they went into His Presence, there were those who testified to the blessing of God by him.

But flat, haven-affording Holland soon had to receive him, and from that easy vantage point, with other exiles, he often looked back, longing and loving, on the Bloody Land. While abroad, godly hands were laid on his head, and he was set apart to the work to which he was surely called, the ministry of the Gospel. After Brown, and Koelman, a Dutch minister, had lifted their hands, the great MacWard kept his upon Cameron's light brown locks, saying " here is the head of a faithful minister and servant of Jesus Christ who shall lose the same for his Master's interest, and it shall be set up before sun and moon in the public view of the world." A Covenanting minister's ordination !

Secretly he got back to Scotland, and soon his name was linked with the very fragrant names of Cargil, Welwood and Hall. Donald Cargil, "blest singular Christian, faithful minister and martyr " ; Henry Hall of Haugh-head, " worthy gentleman, martyr and partaker of Christ's sufferings " ; and " burdened and temperate John Welwood," who, seeing from his cold den his last dawn upon his native hills, said, " Welcome Eternal Light, no more night or darkness for me."

The course of Richard Cameron was swift and bright as that of a blazing meteor. He was fiercely hunted, but kindly housed, and although there was a huge price on his head, there was none that would betray him. Closely sought, he was ever sheltered ; greatly loved, and that unto death, ever with Michael, his brother, by his side. His sermons were full of

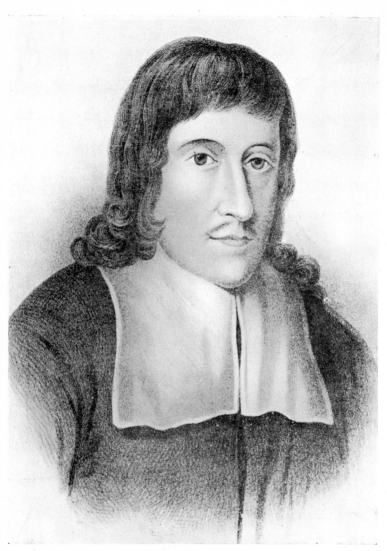

JAMES GUTHRIE

SIGNING THE COVENANT IN GREYFRIARS CHURCHYARD, EDINBURGH

the warm welcoming love of the Lord Jesus Christ for poor helpless sinners : " Will ye take Him ? Tell us what ye say ! These hills and mountains around us witness that we have offered Him to ye this day. Angels are wondering at this offer. They stand beholding with admiration that our Lord is giving ye such an offer this day. They will go up to report at the Throne what is everyone's choice." He preached memorably from such texts as these, Jer. 3, 19, " How shall I put thee among the children ? " Matt. 11, 28, " Come unto Me, all ye that labour and are heavy laden, and I will give you rest ; " Isaiah 32, 2, " And a man shall be as an hiding place from the wind and a covert from the tempest " ; Isaiah 49, 24, " Shall the prey be taken from the mighty, or the lawful captive delivered " ; and John 5,40, " And ye will not come unto Me, that ye might have life." In the midst of this sermon, seeking to make a contract between human hearts and Christ, he fell aweeping, and crowds wept with him, their hearts tendering to the Man of Calvary. As was Cameron's preaching, so was his praying, and his practising. Such as he believed, as believed James Frazer, suffering in the same cause, in his interesting words, " of a Minister's Work and Qualification " : " That which I was called to was, to testify for God, to hold forth His Name and ways to the dark world, and to deliver poor captives of Satan, and bring them to the glorious liberty of the children of God. This I was to make my only employment, to give myself to, and therein to be diligent taking all occasions." And thus he goes on clear in his apprehension as to the greatest calling on earth, and finishing so markedly, " and my own soul to lie at the stake to be forfeit if I failed ; and this commission might have been discharged—though I had never taken a text or preached formally." May we all be delivered from taking a text and preaching formally !

Then came the magnificently brave Sanquhar Declaration,

C

and the savagely intensified hunt of the men of blood.   Less than three weeks before fierce Ayrsmoss, Richard Cameron said, " I shall be but a breakfast to the enemies shortly."   After a day of prayer, twelve days from the end, his word was, " my body shall dung the wilderness within a fortnight."   And " he seldom prayed in a family, or sought a blessing, or gave thanks, but he requested that he might wait with patience till the Lord's time come."   The last Sabbath of his life he was with the dauntless veteran, Donald Cargil, and preached from Psalm 46, 10, " Be still and know that I am God."   The next Sabbath Cargil was preaching from the words, " Know ye not that there is a great man and prince fallen this day in Israel." It was a time of eating of the bread of affliction.

The last week of Richard Cameron's life was lived with about sixty others.   Patrick Walker, the Covenanter Pedlar, the Covenanting John Bunyan, says of them in his unique record, " they were of one heart and soul, their company and converse being so edifying and sweet, and having no certain dwelling-place they stayed together, waiting for further light in that nonsuch juncture of time."   They were somewhat armed, and about twenty of them had horses.   Some may feel that they should not have taken up arms at all.   Many Covenanters themselves felt like this, believing that there was a better testimony to be gained by suffering than by resisting.   Their own outlaw ministers and writers counselled them to be, " as jewels surrounded by the cutting irons," and so, " to seal from your own experience the sweetness of suffering for Christ," since, " there is an inherent glory in suffering for Christ."   But there were many others who, while they could go through much themselves, could not endure seeing others subjected to utmost miseries and cruelties, and were as those when " every man had his sword upon his thigh."   Whatever we feel, we cannot but love them, these rebels so glorious, so brave for God.   It was of them Delta Moir wrote :

" We have no hearth—the ashes lie
        In blackness where they brightly shone ;
    We have no home—the desert sky
        Our covering, earth our couch alone ;
    We have no heritage—depriven
        Of these, we ask not such on earth ;
    Our hearts are sealed ; we seek in Heaven
        For heritage, and home and hearth.

    O Salem, city of the Saints,
        And holy men made perfect ! we
    Pant for Thy Gates, our spirits faint
        Thy glorious golden streets to see ;
    To mark the rapture that inspires
        The ransomed and redeemed by grace,
    To listen to the seraph's lyres
        And meet the angels face to face."

The Lion of the Covenant spent his last night on earth at
Meadowhead Farm, the home of William Mitchell. In the
morning he washed his face and hands in an old stone trough.
On drying himself he looked at his hands, and laying them on
his face, he said to Mrs. Mitchell and her daughter, " This is
their last washing. I have need to make them clean, for there
are many to see them." At this Mrs. Mitchell wept.

That day at about four in the afternoon, the dragoons came
upon that Bible-reading band " in the very desert place of
Ayrsmoss." The Covenanters gathered around their young
leader, with the horsemen on either side of those on foot. He
led them in prayer, appealing three times to the Lord of
Sabaoth, " spare the green, and take the ripe." Looking on
his younger brother, he said to him, " Come Michael, let us
fight it out to the last ; for this is the day that I have longed for,
to die fighting against our Lord's avowed enemies ; and this is
the day that we shall get the crown." To his loved fellows he
said, " Be encouraged all of you, to fight it out valiantly, for all
of you who fall this day I see Heaven's Gates cast wide open to

receive them." Then, " with eyes turned to Heaven, in calm resignation they sang their last song to the God of Salvation."

The dragoons emboldened by greater numbers and better arms attacked at once. The wanderers, as was their wont, defended bravely, and David Hackston says, " The rest of us advanced fast on the enemy, being a strong body of horse coming hard on us, whereupon when we were joined, our horse fired first, and wounded and killed some of them, both horse and foot. Our horse advanced to their faces, and we fired on each other ; I being foremost, after receiving their fire, and finding the horse behind me broken, I then rode in amongst them, and went out at a side without any wrong or wound. I was pursued by several, with whom I fought a good space, sometimes they following me, and sometimes I following them." At last with a treacherous and unfair blow David Hackston was struck down, but, he says, " they gave us all testimony of being brave resolute men." Nine were slain " of that poor party that occasionally met at Ayrsmoss only for the hearing of the Gospel." Among them had flashed to God the dauntless spirit of him known among men as the Lion of the Covenant, Richard Cameron. And Michael, the unseparable, went with him. Most escaped into the wild wide mosses. Six prisoners only were taken. These were William Manuel, John Vallance, John Pollock, David Hackston, John Malcolm, and Archibald Alison. From the severity of his wounds, and from the harsh treatment he received, William Manuel died as he was being carried into the Edinburgh Tolbooth. From the same causes John Vallance died the day following. John Pollock was most cruelly treated, but in the midst of it was steadfast and cheerful, and was banished as a slave to the American Plantations with the marks of his torture still upon him.

*   *   *   *

From whom did the early American slaves wrested from

Africa hear the Gospel ? No doubt from Puritans and Quakers. But such were not fellow slaves. The former lived more in their own settlements, and the latter to their everlasting credit, would not hold slaves. Whosoever got to a Quaker settlement was at once a free man. To the West Indies, Barbadoes and South Carolina many Covenanters were sent as slaves. The accounts of their tragic hell-ships make painful reading. Hundreds of these godly men and women, shipped to be sold as slaves, perished in most terrible conditions through disease, and in fearful storms were drowned miserably battened under hatches. From those who reached the Plantations black slaves heard the Gospel, and thus white-skinned slave and black rejoiced in one common Lord.

In our young years we were rightly familiar with Long-fellow's poem, beginning :

> " Beside the ungathered rice he lay,
> His sickle in his hand,"

but it is possible that it was not always an African who so lay. Now and again it may have been one, who in his last visions saw not himself " once more a king he rode," but who was back once again in fellowship among the hunted " of one heart and one soul."

The Negro Spirituals always have a hearing. The words of worship there united with the moving melody are a living union. But such melodies, it seems, may be sought for in vain in the negroes' own native land, Africa. Whence came they ? Out of something wondrously new, the dark soul meeting with the Light of Life, Christ Jesus ? Yes ! And out of fellowship in His Sufferings, and the fellowship of Christ Jesus in the slaves' sufferings. Yes, no doubt of that. But there are seeming traces of time and melody in these lovely spirituals which are reminiscent of the music of the Old Metrical Psalm singing.

Who can say? At anyrate, these banished men and women carried the message of Redeeming Love to their fellow-slaves of another race.

*　　　*　　　*　　　*

The other three prisoners were executed, David Hackston being shockingly murdered upon the scaffold, and John Malcolm, with Archibald Alison, was hanged. Said John Malcolm, " let His Cause be your cause in weal and woe. O noble Cause! O noble work! O noble Heaven! O noble Christ that makes it to be Heaven and He is the owner of the Work! . . . I lay down my life not as an evildoer, but as a sufferer for Jesus Christ." Said Archibald Alison, " What think ye of Heaven and Glory that are at the back of the Cross? The hope of this makes me look upon pale death as a lovely messenger to me. I bless the Lord for my lot this day . . . . Friends, give our Lord credit; He is aye good, but O! He is good in the day of trial, and He will be sweet company through the ages of Eternity." Of those who escaped from Ayrsmoss, " some wept that they died not that day, but," says Patrick Walker, " those eight who died on the spot with him went ripe and longing for that day and death." The dragoons dug a pit and tumbled the dead into it, after they had cut off the head and hands of Richard Cameron, and the head of John Fowler in mistake for that of Michael Cameron. These were put into a sack to take to the bloodthirsty Council in Edinburgh. In passing through Lanark, the dragoons asked Elizabeth Hope if she would like to buy some calves' heads, and shaking the martyrs' heads out of the bag, they " kicked them up and down the house like footballs," so that the woman fainted.

On reaching Edinburgh, the dragoons put the heads upon halberts with the cry, " there are the heads of traitors, rebels! " One who was there said that he " saw them take Mr. Cameron's head out of the sack; he knew it, being formerly his hearer—

a man of a fair complexion with his own hair, and his face very little altered, and they put a halbert in his blessed mouth out of which had proceeded many gracious words." Robert Murray, as he delivered them to the Council said, " These are the head and hands that lived praying and preaching, and died praying and fighting." And those ghouls of gore paid over the price of the blood of one who died at about the age of his Master.

Before the hangman set head and hands on the bloodstained dried Netherbow Port, the fingers pointing grimly upwards on either side of the head, a hero saint lying in prison was shown them. He was Alan Cameron, Covenanter. The cruel question was asked him, " Do you know them ? " " His son's head and hands which were very fair, being a man of fair complexion like himself." He kissed them saying, " I know them, I know them. They are my son's, my own dear son's. It is the Lord. Good is the will of the Lord, Who cannot wrong me nor mine, but has made goodness and mercy to follow us all our days." A prisoner, head of a broken home, the father of martyred sons and daughter ! It is the answer of the more than conqueror, the sufferer in Christ, full of faith and of the Holy Ghost ; and having the heart full of the power and music of the Good Shepherd Psalm.

> " Goodness and mercy all my life
>   Shall surely follow me ;
> And in God's House forever more
>   My dwelling place shall be."

David Hackston

" . . . . . . They cut the heart from out the living man
And waved it as a flag is waved upon the battle's van ;
And burned it as a beast is burned some idol to appease,
And cast the human ashes round like incense on the breeze,
And they did it in the Name of God !   Where were His lightnings then,
That came not with consuming fire
To light the everlasting pyre
For these blaspheming men ? "

HENRY INGLIS (*Hackston of Rathillet*).

A GENTLEMAN of good family, related to some of the best families in the land, but not in the Family of God ; living in the fresh bloom of early manhood, in the lovely parish of Kilmany, in the Kingdom of Fife, but dead in trespasses and sins, and not in the Kingdom of God—such was David Hackston.   But among the hills he went to hear the homeless wanderers preach, " Peace through the Blood of His Cross," and " Life by His Death," and returned again to his own comfortable home a new man in Christ Jesus, sins all forgiven and having Life Everlasting.   One now in faith with the persecuted and despised, he deliberately became one with them in practice, counting their fellowship " greater riches," his yea and amen one with theirs.   In mountain cave and on bloody field, his heart and hands were in his word, all faithful things, till that cruel day when no word to man was permitted him, and of heart and hands he had none.

Covenanter, turned scented Cavalier, James Sharp, Archbishop of St. Andrews, " and the curse of God with it," the Judas of the Covenant, was hounding to the death the people of the Lord, cutting off " the gangrene of dissent " which was his word for the slaying of the Lord's Anointed.   Lives were being cut off in the dungeon, and stones cast upon them; the waters were overflowing the heads of many, and only Jesus was saying to them, "Be strong, fear not," when some of the hunted turned in their tracks and became hunters. And, one day, while looking for one of Sharp's confederates, they came upon the Archbishop archkiller himself in his grand carriage with equipage driving fair for his own palace towers. And all the way from Edinburgh too where he had been helping to make some hell-hatched laws against the men of the cropped ears, the broken fingers and the mangled limbs. Of James Sharp, Patrick the Pedlar says, "I have often wondered if ever the sun shone upon a man guilty of so many dreadful unheard of acts of wickedness, attended with all aggravating circumstances to make them prodigiously heinous, except his dear brother Judas." And here he was! The maddened band wanted to slay him at once, saying that it was God who had put him into their hands, and had Scriptures to prove it so. Their leader, David Hackston, would take no part in it, saying that he himself had no call to kill the monster. So quickly they chose another leader, Hackston's brother-in-law, Balfour of Kinloch, and, galloping off, came up with the Archbishop's coach on woeful Magus Muir. Calling Sharp Judas and murderer, they dragged him forth, and, with sword and gun, slew him before the eyes of his poor, shrieking, demented daughter. A few days later, Bishop Paterson, the inventor of the thumbscrews, preached his funeral sermon! But as it was a Paterson who, out of hate, invented the thumbscrews, so was it a Paterson, Robert Paterson, "Old Mortality," who, in love for the Covenanters, gave his life to follow over hill, through glen, in mosses, on mountains, and in old country churchyards, cutting the honoured martyr names afresh upon the stones above their poor remains.

And so saints killed saint-killer, but had to be back soon again in their native air on the slopes of Mount Calvary where they were born, where they most truly lived, and best died. Many a pint of innocent blood was death to drink because of James Sharp, murder's advocate, having received his full fee from his client. That of David Hackston was to be drunk very slowly, for surely death never had crueller hands than on the day the life of this merciful man was rung out of him.

With the scattering of the zealous band, David Hackston set off for the West Country to be with honest-hearted Cargil, to whom even in his last hours he bore witness, " I know that the mind of God is with him." With Donald Cargil and others, he read, prayed, fasted and sang, till the glorious Sabbath Field Meeting, which, through the too hurried attack of the cocksure dragoons, became for the Covenanters the victory of Drumclog. Claverhouse himself barely escaped with his wretched life, reserved for doom at Killicrankie. He never forgot nor forgave Drumclog.

Tragic and pathetic Bothwell Brig came on with the fifteen thousand against the four thousand, and the righteous " hagged and hashed, and their blood ran like water," followed by the queues for the gallows, the tortures, and the transportations under popish captains to slavery. At Bothwell, David Hackston commanded his godly three hundred on the left side of the bridge. He appealed in vain not to be asked to retreat, and was amongst the last to leave the stricken field, escaping into the kindly folds of the Covenanters' mantle—the everlasting hills, where, with a great price set for his capture, he joined Richard Cameron and his men of One Accord. One door only was open to them—the way to the Throne, by prayer or by presence. The Covenanters' colours were rightly chosen, scarlet and blue.

For a year, among the shades and mists of the glens and moors, they held sweet fellowship together, and never was there one who would betray that praying group of rebels glorious. But, on a summer day on the lone Ayrsmoss, they sang their last

song to the God of their so prized Salvation, and their leader
Richard Cameron, the Lion of the Covenant, prayed his last
prayer, crying, " Spare the green and take the ripe," and was
gathered in as a sheaf of gold in harvest. David Hackston by
his side, till Cameron fell, fought with superb horsemanship
among the King's Troopers, but, his horse sticking in a bog, he
dismounted to fight it out on foot with David Ramsay, an old
acquaintance, when three horse troopers coming at him from
behind meanly cut him down, and he was made prisoner. "The
field was theirs," he said, " but they paid for it. We compelled
them to give us the testimony that we were resolute and brave."

With badly bleeding head wounds, from which he thought
he might die, and with a few other badly wounded sufferers, he
was stripped to not even having shoes upon his feet, and set
upon a barebacked horse, and taken away towards Edinburgh.
Coming to Lanark, the brutal dragoons played with the hashed-
off heads of Cameron and Fowler as if they had been footballs.
Here also the prisoners were examined by General Tam
Dalziel, the " Muscovite Brute," who, not getting satisfactory
answers to his questions, threatened to roast Hackston alive.
The small, melancholy, shameful procession arrived near
Edinburgh, and by the hangman were led into the city. Hackston, his hands tied, sat facing the tail of his white barebacked
horse, with his feet tied below its belly. The other five were
harled along on some kind of an iron grid or tumbril, William
Manuel, one of them, blessedly reaching Emmanuel's Land
just as they reached the prison gates. The head of Cameron,
all the while, was carried before them aloft upon a halbert, and
the head of John Fowler carried in a sack by a boy.

David Hackston was immediately brought before the
Council, questioned, and found to be true to Christ, the
Covenant, and the Fellowship, even to saying that he thought
Archbishop Sharp's death to be no murder. Such is loyal

fellowship—having no part in the act but a share in the sentence if need be. Some of the questions put to him he refused to answer, but requested that he might speak a little to give a testimony. This was granted, and he said, " Ye know that youth is a folly, and I acknowledge that in my younger years I was too much carried down with the flood of it ; but that inexhaustible Fountain of Goodness and Grace of God which is free and great, hath reclaimed me, and as a firebrand hath plucked me out of the claws of Satan, and now I stand here before you as a prisoner of Jesus Christ for adhering to His Cause and Interest, which has been sealed with the blood of many worthies who have suffered in these lands, and have witnessed to the truths of Christ these few years bygone. And I do own all the testimonies given by them, and desire to put in my mite among theirs, and am not only willing to seal it with my blood, but also to seal it with the sharpest tortures that you can imagine."

In prison he wrote four letters : one to his loving sister, one to a gentlewoman of his acquaintance, and two to a Christian friend. Here are a few sentences from them, " Oh, that preachers would preach repentance, and professors would exhort one another to mourn in secret, and together, because of their sin, and with their mourning would believe, for these are very consistent together . . . It was cast up to me both at the Council and here that there were not two hundred in the nation to own our course. I answered at both times that the Cause of Christ had been often owned by fewer . . . I think I dare not misbelieve, but when fear assaults me I think there is a voice saying to me, fear not . . . I am frail, but Christ is strong. I have His Promise of through-bearing . . . If the free grace of God be glorified in me, ought not all to praise Him ? "

A few days more and he was before his merciless judges for the last time, and was asked if he had anything more to say.

He answered, " What I have said I will seal." By reason of his wounds, they thought that he might die if tortured, so they asked him to sit down to receive his sentence. He did so willingly, but told them that they were all murderers. Sentence of death was then passed upon him, and what a death sentence ! It is clear from the old records that the manner of his execution was framed before his last trial. It stands against his judges till this day. Here is the sentence in all its stark savagery : " That his body be drawn backward on a hurdle to the Cross of Edinburgh ; that there be a high scaffold erected a little above the Cross, where in the first place his right hand is to be struck off, and after some time his left hand ; that he is to be hanged up and cut down alive, his bowels to be taken out, and his heart to be shown by the hangman to the people, then his heart and his bowels to be burned in a fire prepared for that purpose on the scaffold, that afterward his head be cut off, and his body divided into four quarters, his head to be fixed on the Netherbow, one of his quarters with both his hands to be affixed at St. Andrews, another quarter at Glasgow, a third at Leith, a fourth at Burnt-island ; that none presume to be in mourning for him, nor any coffin brought, that no person be suffered to be on the scaffold with him save the two bailies, the executioner and his servants ; that he be allowed to pray to God Almighty, but not to speak to the people ; that the heads of Cameron and Fowler be affixed on the Netherbow ; that Hackston's and Cameron's heads be affixed on higher poles than the rest."

Already dying from his ghastly wounds, he was led away to suffer. While great crowds looked on, there was done upon him, by the hangman, a gross, painful barbarity not mentioned in his sentence. Then he endured with firmness and patience the cutting off of his hands, but, the hangman having taken such a long time to hack off his right hand, he asked that his left hand might be taken off at the joint, which was done. With a pulley he was then pulled to the top of the gallows, and, when choked a little, was let down alive. The hangman then with a sharp knife opened his breast, and, putting in his hand, pulled out his heart. It fell upon the scaffold and moved there. The hangman picked it up on the point of his knife, and, carrying it around the scaffold, he showed it to the people saying, " here is the heart of a traitor." Patrick Walker says that it fluttered upon the knife. The rest of the sentence was duly carried out, and the free Grace of God was glorified in David Hackston, so that whoever thinks of him must think of his Lord and Saviour, Jesus, too.

About a fortnight later two of his fellowsoldier peasant saints followed him. John Malcolm and Archibald Alison, by the rope, glorified God in the Grassmarket. Said John Malcolm, " I bless the Lord that ever He made choice of me, who was a miserable sinner, to lay down my life for His Cause." Said Archibald Alison, " For my part I am glad that He calls me away after this manner, for which I desire with my soul to bless Him for His kindness to me in taking this method, and this way, with such a wretched sinner as I am, who deserves nothing, nothing but wrath and only wrath." So they joined their fellow soldier in Christ, David Hackston, with him to get

> " a standing there and place
> Among the beams, which crown the Face
> Of Him, Who died to part
> Sin and my heart."

John Brown

" The child on the moss she laid
And she stretched the cold limbs of the dead,
And drew the eyelid's shade,
And bound the corpse's shattered head,
And shrouded the martyr in his plaid ;
And where the dead and living slept,
Sate in the wilderness and wept."

HENRY INGLIS (*The Death of John Brown*).

THE simple name of John Brown is familiar and famous.
literature, history and religion all witness that more than
one " John Brown's body lies amouldering in his grave while his
soul goes marching on." Several Covenanting martyrs bore
this honoured name, and among his godly namesakes, John
Brown of Priesthill has a humble, gracious place. Though but
a workman peasant believer, he was a type of manhood at its
best, full orbed in Christ, ascending the hill of the Lord with
clean hands and a pure heart.

Like many another Covenanter, he came from the Shire of
Ayr, the land of Burns ; by him famed in lovely human song as
long as human things endure ; the land of Murdoch, of coal-gas
discovery ; of MacAdam who has done so much for our roads ;
of Baird, discoverer of television ; and of Fleming, discoverer
of penicillin, probably yet to be one of the best boons to man-
kind. Ayrshire is the old Land of Kyle, famous for its Lollard
preaching and staunch adherence to Reformation principles.
Dear to its exiles, even when within sight of The Better Country,
one of them said to old Adam Sanderson after the cruel day of
Rullion Green, where he had received his death wounds,
" Bury me within sight of my Ayrshire Hills." The Pentland
farmer saw him pass into the Presence of his Dearly Loved
Saviour, " free frae the toil and the moil and the mirk, and the

tyrant's cursed pride," and, taking up the poor broken clay upon his back, he carried the nameless lad and buried him on a ridge from where one can see the dim outline of the low Ayrshire Hills.

John Brown was the very close friend of both Richard Cameron, the Lion of the Covenant, and of Alexander Peden, " Puir Auld Sandy," the Prophet of the Covenant. Cameron he looked upon as the very voice of God for his generation, and quoted him as such ; while the fellowship on earth of Peden was to him a taste of the joys of the world to come. When Brown fell, Peden referred to him as " a clear shining light, the greatest Christian I ever conversed with." He had married " the carrier of Calvary " to Isabel Weir in 1682, and after the simple Puritan ceremony had said to Isabel, " Ye have a good man to be your husband, but ye will not enjoy him long ; prize his company, and keep linen by you to be his winding sheet, for ye will need it when ye are not looking for it, and it will be a bloody one." A Covenanting wedding ! The Covenanter's deepest joys ever carried the shadow of the Cross.

John Brown of Priesthill was poor. Till the day he died he never owned much more than twenty sheep and a cow. His small crofting cottage is now no more. On every side stretch miles upon miles of melancholy moorlands with the heather creeping lovingly around his memorial stone. He was buried where he fell, just outside his own door. One need but stand in the silence there to hear again the humble little family at worship, and John Brown singing his last psalm, the psalm of the " dull misty morning." It sings in one's heart till it fills earth and sky with its music, till it blends and is lost in the greatest psalm of all—the Song of the Redeemed in the Great Day of Triumph singing " Worthy is the Lamb that was slain."

By all accounts he was rarely gifted, and carried a brilliant intellect yielded to Christ. He had his own rustic school of

JOHN BROWN

THE COVENANTERS

theology, and his classes were attended by youths from miles around. Three of these class members sealed their testimonies with their blood, and their leader had often times to flee. An impediment in his speech had made him give up the thought of being a Covenanting minister, but here was his own Bible School where he taught youth to resist unto blood, striving against sin. In the summer time they held their classes in the sheepfold, and in the winter they sat around the peat fire in the kitchen. We rightly look upon John Brown of Priesthill as being one of our first founders of Bible Classes and Sunday Schools. Oh, that Eternity might stage for us some of the holy scenes of time ! Who would not like to see the Bible School at Priesthill with John Brown in his class of peasant students, candidates for martyrdom ?

How well one can imagine them going over Walter Smith's " Twenty-Two Steps of Defection," and " Rules for Society Meetings," and praying God to help them to follow out faithfully, with all other members of the United Societies, the teaching set down therein by that God-lit soul ! How greatly at heart the Covenanters had the Church, the Jew and the Unreached Heathen. What would they have done had they had present opportunity ? Though hunted like wild beasts, the Spirit of God testifies that they had the mind of Christ. Here is a small part out of their Rules for Society Meetings : " As it is the undoubted duty of all to pray for the coming of Christ's kingdom, so all that love our Lord Jesus Christ in sincerity, and know what it is to bow a knee in good earnest, will long and pray for the out-making of the gospel promises to His Church in the latter days, that King Christ would go out upon the white horse of the gospel, conquering and to conquer, and make a conquest of the travail of His soul, that it may be sounded that the kingdoms of the world are become His, and His Name called upon from the rising of the sun to its going down.

D

(1) That the old casten of Israel would never be forgotten, especially in these meetings. That the promised day of their ingrafting might be hastened ; and that dead weight of blood removed off them, that their fathers took upon them and upon their children, that have sunk them down to hell, upwards of seventeen hundred years.

(2) That the Lord's written and preached word may be sent with power to enlighten the poor Pagan world, living in black perishing darkness without Christ and the knowledge of His Name . . . that they would love, sympathise, and pray for one another in secret, and in their families who have them, and weep when any member weeps, and rejoice with all such as are joined in this society communion which is the strictest of all communions ; and before they go to their meetings everyone would be importunate with the Lord to go with them and meet with them, that it may be for the better and not for the worse, and with all such meetings." So this moving paper runs on to its close, " Rules and Directions anent Private Christian Meetings for Prayer and Conference to Mutual Edification, and to the Right Management of the Same." With other four martyrs, the writer of it, Walter Smith, was hanged at the Cross of Edinburgh, 27th July, 1681. The other four were Donald Cargil, James Boig, William Cuthil, and William Thomson— " and all their five heads hashed and hagged off upon the scaffold by the common man's Bloody Axe : the first three heads fixed upon the Netherbow-port, and the last two upon the West-port." Says Patrick Walker, speaking of Cargil, " he wrote that by virtue of the mercies of God, and merits of Christ he had a conscience as quiet and calm as if he had never sinned," and continues, " When he came to the scaffold and foot of the ladder he blessed the Lord with uplifted hands that he was thus near the crown ; and when setting his foot upon the ladder to go up to embrace the bloody rope, he said, ' The Lord knows I

go up this ladder with less fear, confusion or perturbation of mind, than ever I entered a pulpit to preach.' He was first turned over. Mr. Smith, as he did cleave to him in love and unity in life, so he died with his face upon his breast." So went to Heaven, young, twenty-six years old, " singular worthy, and faithful-unto-death Mr. Walter Smith," with a heart filled for World-wide Evangelization.

* * * *

The year 1685 was a terrible year in a terrible era. The Killing Time reeked reddest then. The author of Robinson Crusoe, Daniel Defoe, one of the most painstaking and sympathetic writers on the Covenanters, " fixes on the barbarities of this year to support his opinion that the Scottish persecution was worse than that of the Roman Emperors and Popish Inquisitors." It was also from this year that Lord Macauley selected his history of a single fortnight to show the horrors of government under a Stuart king. Long is the roll of the names of the martyrs—the lashed to the hooks, the burned by the match, the redhot iron branded, the starved to death, the bone mangled and crushed, the earclipped, the banished, the wounded and torn by bullet and knife. But as the horrors are bestial and brutal, so are the testimonies tender and spirit quickening. The Covenanters died praying and praising. While their persecutors lived in sin, they prepared themselves for Heaven, deeming themselves blessed forever because blessed of the Lord.

In April of that year, the hawks that harry were searching hill, glen, moss and moor, looking for two shepherds of the flocks, the man Peden and the boy Renwick, and one night Peden arrived at the holy haven of Priesthill, stayed the night and went away again very early in the morning, saying in his prophetic way, " it is a fearful morning, a dark misty morning." Between five and six next morning, after family worship, John

Brown with his young nephew, John Browning, went out to cut some peats. They had not long been gone when, in the midst of a dark and thick mist, Claverhouse with three troops of horse, looking for Peden came upon them. They ran, but were caught and brought back to Priesthill for cruel cross-examination. The bare-footed lad was shamefully treated. Claverhouse in a letter relates his own cruelty to the boy. He was questioned much, sentenced to death, ordered to pray, and faced the firing squad. Bloody Clavers then reprieved him, saying that he would hand him over to justice, and that he would make an appeal for him. Captain Drummond was to have charge of him. Alas! it seems from history that Drummond hanged the laddie with the bare feet. The word of Clavers was like himself—just Clavers.

Priesthill was ransacked and so called treasonable papers were found. Brown was questioned. His stammering disappeared, and he answered every question so solidly and distinctly that Claverhouse asked his base guides if ever they had heard him preach. " No, no," they said, " he was never a preacher." " Well," said he, " if he has never preached, much has he prayed in his time. Go to your prayers," he shouted, " for you shall immediately die." The peasant went to his knees and began to pray, but three times Claverhouse interrupted him, and then completely stopped him as John Brown interceded asking God to spare a remnant. " I gave you leave to pray," he bawled, " and you have begun to preach." The Covenanter turned upon his knees, " Sir," he said, " you know neither the nature of preaching nor praying that calls this preaching," and looking to God, finished his last prayer. " Take goodbye of your wife and children," said " the pitiful creature," Bonnie Dundee—the Ugly, man of blood. Isabel Brown was standing by with her child in her arms, and another child of John Brown's first wife by her side. He came to her saying, " Now Isabel, the day is come that I told you would come when I spoke to you first of marrying me." She said, " Indeed, John, I can willingly part with you." " That is all I desire," he replied. " I have no more to do but to die. I have been in happy case to meet with death for so many years." He kissed her and his children, saying that he wished Blood-bought and Gospel-promised blessings to be multiplied upon them, and Claverhouse roughly broke in, ordering six dragoons to shoot him. As he stood before them their hearts were moved ; they lowered their muskets and refused to fire. But the killer of many wildly unbelted his pistol, and hastily walking up to John Brown, placed it to his head, and blew his brains out, scattering them upon the ground. Looking at his ghastly work with a sardonic smile, he turned to Isabel saying, " What do you think, of your fine husband now ? " and through her sad tears she bravely answered, " I ever thought much good of him, and more than ever now." " It were but justice to lay you beside him," he returned. Said she, " If you were permitted, I doubt not but your cruelty would go that length. But then, how will ye answer to God for this morning's work ? " Arrogantly, he blustered, " To man I can be answerable. And as for God, I shall take Him into my own hand ! " He then mounted his horse and haughtily rode off at the head of his troops. He later confessed that if he gave himself liberty to think of it, he could never forget John Brown's prayer.

Isabel Brown set her child upon the ground, gathered up her husband's brains, tied up his head, straightened his body, and covering it with a plaid, sat down and wept. Thus was she found by Widow Jean Brown, whose own husband and two sons had been slain in the same great cause.

About ten miles away Peden had been in the fields all night. Very early in the morning he called at a country cottage where lived a praying family named Muirhead, and asking them for fellowship in prayer, he began to pour out his heart in melting crying to God, " Lord," he cried with all the poignant pathos of the helpless wanderer, " Lord, when wilt Thou avenge Brown's blood ! Oh, let Brown's blood be precious in Thy sight." John Muirhead enquired from him what he meant. " What do I mean," said this strange unusual saint of God, " I mean that Claverhouse has been at the Priesthill, and has cruelly murdered John Brown. His corpse is lying at the end of his house, his poor wife sitting by it, with not a soul to speak comfortably to her."

It was on a May morning, the first day of summer in the Killing Time, that Isabel Weir offered up the priceless jewel of her life, John Brown, her husband. He went swiftly to company he had often longed for, where he would be much at home. She lived on in brave, godly, covenanting widowhood, bringing up her children, succouring the godly, and comforting the mourner with the comfort wherewith she had been comforted of God.   *   *   *   *

" The Book of the Intricacies of My Heart, the Memoirs of James Frazer, Covenanter," is not as well known as " Grace Abounding to the Chief of Sinners," but maybe it ought to bet Himself a sufferer, he testifies to the consolations and comfors. of the Lord. Says he, " The greatest consolations do attend the greatest tribulations, 2 Cor. 1, 5-6. The first brunt of the cross is saddest and sharpest ; no affliction for the present seemeth joyous but grievous. Great outward troubles, whether personal or on public accounts, quicken and revive our appre- hensions of eternity, and always do us good, though not alike good to all, nor so sensibly. Yet no cross but we get some good of it. I found it very hard to appear before councils and carry rightly. We seek rather to save ourselves in any lawful way than to give testimony for Christ." And he closes his great memoirs in a way that reaches us all till He comes, " There is a large allowance for sufferers for righteousness ; but many live not upon their allowance, and therefore look so ill upon it."

Margaret MacLachlan and Margaret Wilson

" Long had they loved as Christians love—
Those two so soon to die,
And each the other greeted first,
With weeping silently.
The matron wept that that young life
So timelessly must cease ;
The maiden that that honoured head
Must not go down in peace.

But soon, O soon, it passed away
The coward thought and base,
And each looked humbly, thankfully,
Into the other's face.
" Mother, He rules the awful sea
With all its waters wild."
" The many waters are His Voice
Of love to thee, my child."

Harriet Stuart Menteith.

LIKE some other Protestant institutions, many of our Orange
Lodges have lost their pristine spiritual power. The
Spirit now gone, the reading of the Holy Scriptures and the
saying of prayers are lifeless formalities. We are left with but
a round of social fellowship and a name. Yet an Orange Walk
is a stirring sight ! The fluttering banners, trimmed in their
ribbons of orange and blue, bring to mind the Scripture, " as
glorious as an army with banners." And as the banner,
" Solway Martyrs," is carried past with its vivid picture of the
faithful Margarets dying amid the swirling waters, what heart
has not felt thankful for what they died to win—freedom to
worship God.

*   *   *   *

Before a very savage court, at Wigtown, April 13th, 1685,
stood four female prisoners. They all had refused Prelacy and

the oath of Abjuration, which latter made its swearer own the Church of God to be a department of the State. Their indictment was for rebellion, attending of field meetings, and meetings for worship within doors—twenty of each ! Finding them guilty, bestial Grierson of Lagg, a violent persecutor of the Covenanters, ordered that they should receive sentence while on their knees. They refused to kneel, but were brutally forced to, and were held down while sentences were pronounced upon them : Margaret MacLachlan, widow, seventy years of age, to die by drowning ; Margaret Maxwel, serving maid, twenty years of age, to be flogged publicly through the streets of Wigtown three days in succession, and to stand each of these days for an hour in the stocks ; Margaret Wilson, farmer's daughter, eighteen years of age, to die by drowning ; Agnes Wilson, sister of Margaret, thirteen years of age, her father, Gilbert Wilson, to pay £100 bond for her.

Margaret MacLachlan was of a manner of life Christlike and very highly esteemed by her fellow Christians. Patrick Walker says, " those of her intimates said to me that she was a Christian of deep exercise through most of her life, and of high attainments and great experiences in the ways of godliness." She was much harassed by the persecutors, and one day, while she was upon her knees worshipping God with her family around her, a party of dragoons arrived, arrested her, and put her in prison, where she suffered much from want of food, fire and bed. She had not even light to read the Holy Scriptures. All her record is in these words, " Faithful unto death."

Patrick the Pedlar tells us also that when Margaret Maxwel was an old woman he talked with her, and she told him, " she was then a prisoner with them and expected the same sentence, but she was ordained to be scourged through the town of Wigtown by the hand of the common hangman three days successively, and to stand each day one hour in juggs (stocks).

All which was done. But such was the cruelty of these days that all who retained anything of humanity toward their fellow-creatures abhorred such barbarity; so that all the three days that the foresaid Margaret was punished and exposed, there was scarce one open door or window to be seen in the town of Wigtown, and no boys or girls looking on. The officers and hangman enquiring if they should shorten the hour, she said, " No ; let the clock go on." She was neither wearied nor ashamed. The hangman was very tender to her."

Margaret and Agnes Wilson, daughters of rich Gilbert Wilson, farmer in Glenvernock, had with their brother Tom, of sixteen years of age, refused to conform to vain religion. Searched for, they fled and lived among the wild mountains, bogs and caves, youthful, vagrant, holy things. Their parents were charged on their highest peril that they should neither house them, give food to them, speak to them nor see them. The country people were ordered by law to pursue them even as did the rude soldiery.

Their parents were yet to suffer much for the godliness of their children. For several years at a time, as many as a hundred soldiers were quartered on them. Heavy fines were exacted, and courts were imposed, meaning a once a week horse journey of many miles, which went on for three years, and Gilbert Wilson died at last in utter poverty. His wife was supported and cared for by friends, and when Tom returned from soldiering in the army of William of Orange, there was nothing left to return to.

During February, the two girls left Tom among the snows of the mountains and came down secretly to see some friends in Wigtown, where some one asked them to drink the king's health. That they could not do, they said, for it was not warranted by Scripture, and belied Christian moderation. Thus they were recognised, arrested and thrust into prison in the Thieves Hole, as if they had been ferocious criminals. There they lay until their trial on April 13th, when with the widow and the serving-lass, they heard their sentences, and judged it an honour to suffer for their Saviour's sake.

Gilbert Wilson paid the heavy bond for his little Agnes, and set off on horseback to Edinburgh with an appeal for Margaret. But, by the time he returned, the sad tragedy had taken place, and she was where there is " no more sea."

*   *   *   *

John Brown, the Carrier of Calvary, "won Hame," on May morning.   Next day, beneath the early summer sun, these two ladies of the Covenant, Margaret Wilson and Margaret MacLachlan, were wrestling in their cruel heavy swellings of Jordan.   They were summer and winter in the Glorious Cause, Margaret of the flaxen hair, and Margaret of the grey.   From the darksome prisonhouse, the soldiers took them to the banks of the Blednoch Burn which fills with Solway from the sea when the swift running tide comes in.   Two long wooden stakes had been fixed deeply in the bed of the burn.   The farther out one, nearer the oncoming waves, was for Mother Margaret ; and the other, nearer to the land, was for Margaret the Maid.

We never read of any word the old saint spoke.   It appears that, sick at heart and disappointed with madly cruel humanity, she turned to unending communion with the Lord.   " It is needless to speak to that damned old bitch," they rudely cried, " let her go to hell," and they tied her roughly fast to her leafless but fruitful tree.   So came the hungry waters up and up, every wave splashing death, until she was choking in their cold, cold grasp.   As she struggled, before she became a poor limp thing lying in the swirling flood, they said to young Margaret, " what do you think of her now ? "   " Think ! I see Christ wrestling there," said she.   " Think ye that we are sufferers ?   No ; it is Christ in us, for He sends none a warfare at His own charges."

The waters were now around her, and she began to sing a plaintive melody she had often sung among the hills when the fellowship of the hunted worshipped God. In it the young heart communed with the most High. It was Psalm 25 from the seventh verse :

> " My sins and faults of youth
> Do Thou O Lord forget :
> After Thy mercy think on me,
> And for Thy goodness great.
> God good and upright is :
> The way He'll sinners show ;
> The meek in judgment He will guide
> And make His path to know."

To the Covenanter the Bible was the visible earnest of the New Jerusalem, " that great city, the holy Jerusalem, descending out of Heaven from God, having the glory of God : and her light was like unto a stone most precious, even like a jasper stone, clear as crystal." Her treasure with her, Margaret Wilson opened it up for the last time, to see the precious jewels there. She read aloud from the Eighth Chapter of Romans, in full assurance of faith of the Glory soon to be. " Whom He justified them He also glorified ; " and, convinced of His throughbearing to His Praise, " we are more than conquerors through Him that loved us. For I am persuaded that neither death nor life, nor angels, nor principalities, nor powers, nor things present, nor things to come, nor height, nor depth, nor any other creature, shall be able to separate us from the love of God, which is in Christ Jesus our Lord." The cold waves dashed over her head. Loosely tied, the soldiers pulled her out of the water, and, when she could speak, they asked her to do what the Covenanter could not do—pray for the King, " as he is supreme over all persons and causes, ecclesiastic as well as civil," a blasphemous usurping of the prerogative of Christ as Head of the Church, an arrogant claim which no Covenanter would admit. "Pray for the King," they cried! She murmured that she wished the Salvation of all men, and the damnation of none. They dashed her under the water and pulled her out again. "Oh; Margaret, say it," pleaded some. "Lord give him repentance, forgiveness and salvation, if it be Thy Holy Will," she whispered. Grierson of Lagg, in wild, impatient passion cried, "Damned bitch, we do not want such prayers. Tender her the oaths." She groaned, "No! No! no sinful oaths for me. I am one of Christ's children. Let me go." And they brutally flung her back into the waters, where she died a virgin martyr of eighteen summers.

Their dear dust lies in Wigtown Old Churchyard. It is but a few yards from where they died. The dust of several other martyred Covenanters lies near them.

* * * *

Among the Covenanters, the greatly suffering roll of women who laboured in the Gospel is a very large one. They truly loved Him, and loved not their lives unto the death. And as they comported themselves in the prisons, in the slaveships, and in the waters, so did they also upon the scaffold.

Isabel Alison and Marion Harvie, two young hearts alive unto God and dead to the world, were tried together upon the one indictment, and executed on the same day together, after singing the 23rd Psalm and, a little later, the 84th Psalm, to the mellowed tune of Martyrs, resplendent with the dew of the field, the love of the heart, and the blood of the gallows tree. By every word and act, they glorified their Saviour; and their written and spoken testimonies minister grace. Wrote Isabel, "what shall I say to the commendation of Christ and His Cross? I bless the Lord He has made my prison a palace to me. And what am I that He should have dealt thus with me?

I have looked greedylike to such a lot as this, but still thought it was too high for me when I saw how vile I was." Wrote Marion, " Now farewell, lovely and sweet Scriptures, which were aye my comfort in the midst of all my difficulties! Farewell faith! Farewell hope! Farewell wanderers, who have been comfortable to my soul, in the hearing of them commend Christ's love! Farewell brethren! Farewell sisters! Farewell Christian acquaintances! Farewell sun, moon and stars! And, now, welcome my lovely, heartsome Christ Jesus, into Whose hands I commit my spirit throughout all Eternity. I may say few and evil have the days of the years of my life been, I being about twenty years of age."

The simple word of appreciation for Isabel and Marion from Alexander Peden was, "they were twa honest worthy lassies." Honesty and honour are of one heart, an old pilgrim power like faith, and hope, and love. " They were twa honest worthy lassies " and in them grace reigned.

> " Yonder in joy the sheaves we bring,
>   Whose seed was sown on earth in tears ;
> There in our Father's house we sing
>   The song too sweet for mortal ears.
> Sorrow and sighing all are past
> And pain and death are fled at last,
> There with the Lamb of God we dwell.
> He leads us to the crystal river,
> He wipes away all tears forever
> What there is ours no tongue can tell."

John Nisbet

" and no more
The assembled people dared in face of day,
To worship God, or even at the dead
Of night, save when the wintry storm raged fierce,
And thunder peals compelled the men of blood
To couch within their dens ; then, dauntlessly,
The scattered few would meet, in some deep dell
By rock oer canopied, to hear the voice,
Their faithful pastor's voice ; he by the gleam
Of sheeted lightning, oped the Sacred Book,
And words of comfort spake."

JAMES GRAHAME (*The Sabbath*).

THE night had been dark and long, but when Wycliffe arose, the Morning Star of the Reformation, there were watchers also in Scotland who hastened to his rising, and gathered gold in his shining. One of those was Murdoch Nisbet, of Kyle, who, greatly enriched in the free grace of God, left the miserable hovel of Popery for large room in the Family of God among the first British Protestants, the Lollards.

Threatening storm clouds gathering, he went overseas, taking with him a very treasured manuscript New Testament, and returned when a brighter day was promised. But the storms broke again on all not sheltered by Rome, and Kennedy and Russell, two of Murdoch Nisbet's colleagues, perished in the hell-heated martyr fires of Glasgow.

Murdoch dug deep, and built a vault below his house where he lived a life of prayer. Here he continually read his handwritten New Testament and taught its great doctrines to learners in Christ. With them he eventually went forth boldly preaching the Gospel. Thus, till Glory, continued Murdoch Nisbet.

To Alexander, his son, both in the flesh and in the Spirit, he left his precious Manuscript. Alexander lived in its power, and left it to his son James, a man much taught of the Lord, and greatly strengthened by his helpmeet, Janet Gibson, whose praise in the churches continued through many years. She died young, leaving two children, Mary and John, who saw their father through his long widowed days bend low over the Word of God, and then go Home. To big, strong, broad-shouldered John, soldier of the Thirty Years War, passed the loved manuscript New Testament.

On his return from the wars, John Nisbet married Margaret Law. They settled down comfortably enough until 1661 when King Charles and his counterfeit Protestants drew aside from Reformation principles, whereupon John and Margaret were found among the godly bands who renewed their covenant with God in *the* Covenant.

The Killing Time came on and the military might of Britain prowled the land with a devouring mouth given to it by the devil. Once more, John Nisbet was a soldier. But with no bright gay uniform now ; just the Lowland peasant hodden grey sometimes splashed with living red. No proudly marshalled ranks, nor blast of enlivening trumpets now, but the thinned ranks of the wanderers and their speaking to one another in the silences by imitated call of beast and bird. Such could but win one battle, but it the real one—the victory of faith.

Came Pentland Fight cold and bitter, and, while many fell to die, he fell to live, but with seventeen ugly wounds, from which it took him a year to recover. Stripped naked, he was left for dead upon the field, but, in the chilly wet November night, he crawled away to safety.

Drumclog and Bothwell Battles followed where he got the testimony that he comported himself as a valiant soldier and as

a true Christian.   From the Bothwell defeat he got away, and
the vindictive dragoons, not finding him, made homeless his
wife and children who began their wanderings " in deserts, and
in mountains, and in dens and caves of the earth."   But as
Margaret Law was at the beginning of her sore suffering when
the steel was pointed at her breast, and the pistol was at the ready,
so was she till the end, faithful.   For four years she and her
children battled on, and, on a cold December day, she sank low
among the straw of a sheep cot never to rise again.   Eight days
she lay, her children by her, and then fell asleep in Jesus.
Strangers to the daytime came out with the nightshadows, laid
her in the earth, and faded away again.   News came to John
Nisbet, and, arriving eight days later, he entered the " sheep
cot where was no light or fire but that of a candle, no bed but
that of straw, no stool but the ground to sit on."   Friends were
putting his little daughter in her rude coffin.   Stooping down,
he kissed her tenderly, saying, " Religion does not make us void
of natural affection, but we should be sure it runs in the channel
of sanctified submission to the will of God, of whom we have
our being."   Turning to a corner where two of his sons lay in a
burning fever, he spoke to them but they did not know him.
He groaned saying, " Naked came I into the world and naked I
must go out of it.   The Lord is making my passage easy."
One of the friends said to him, " I hope ye know who hath done
this ?"   But the Covenanter's eyes were ever on God, and
John Nisbet answered as one whose thought was taken up in
profound and inaccessible mystery, passing all second causes,
" I know that He hath done it that makes all things work
together for the good of them who love Him and keep His Way,
even He who first loved us, and this is my comfort.   Also it
doth comfort me very much that my wife whom ye have already
buried out of my sight bears the mouth that never bade me do
that that might hurt my conscience notwithstanding of all the

DONALD   CARGILL

CONDEMNED COVENANTERS BEING TAKEN DOWN
THE WEST BOW, EDINBURGH

troubles she met with on my account. On the contrary, when I was telling her at any time, I dare not do such and such a thing she would have said, ' Well then, see that ye do it not, come of me and my bairns what will. God lives, we need not be afraid, and if ye, they and I were once fairly in Emmanuel's Land, we would be richly made up.' I bless God who gave me such a wife, and I bless Him that He hath taken her again." To Stonehouse Kirkyard they carried his dear child, he bearing her head all the way, and, at midnight, she was laid in close upon her mother's breast. Quickly, he went off again into hiding. The troops got notice of his being about but they found neither him, his sons, nor the graves of his womenfolk.

For about two years more he was among the hillmen and wrote his Large Testimony to Truth, in case he was killed in the fields. A huge price was offered for his capture, and blood-drinkers were eager to get it.

So came the day when he and three others met together for prayer and business, and, as wrote his son James, " it pleased God they were seen." Forty dragoons came upon them and a fierce fight took place in a byre. Shots all spent, with the stocks of their muskets they fought the soldiers, till, the commander ordering the place to be set ablaze, they came out into the open and fought bravely there. The leader of the dragoons, Captain Robert Nisbet, was a relative of Covenanter John Nisbet, and, seeing the possibility of a rich prize, he called for taking him alive. John Nisbet had seven severe wounds, and the other three were badly wounded, but they fought on till all of them were beaten to the ground and made prisoners. Redcoat Nisbet, gloating over his captives, in front of his relation's face, shot his brave fellow Covenanters, Peter Gemmall, George Woodburn, and John Ferguson. Speaking to John Nisbet, the butcher asked what he now thought of himself and his circumstances. Nisbet replied, " I think as

E

well of Christ and His Cause as ever, and not at all the worse for what I suffer. Only I grieve and think myself at a loss that I am left in time when my three dear brethren are gone to Heaven, whom ye have wickedly murdered." He was told that he would have a worse death, and he was taken away on his painful journey to Edinburgh where at his trials he made noble answer for his faith. He told his judges there that he was more afraid to lie than to die, and that he was as willing to give his life as they were to take it. Sentence of death being pronounced upon him, he blessed and praised God that he was counted worthy to suffer for Christ's sake.

He was in prison very cruelly treated, having a load of irons on him of seven stones weight, and not able to move much because of his terrible wounds. But all the time he was filled with inexpressible joy and continually witnessed to strong inward assurance and assistance from the Holy Spirit. He testified, " It has pleased Him to give such real impression of unspeakable glory as without constant and immediate supports trom the Giver will certainly overwhelm me. This frail tabernacle is not able to hold up under what I now feel."

A few days before he was hanged, he was so transported while at worship with other prisoners that he called aloud in prayer, " O for Friday ! O for Friday ! O Lord, give patience to wait Thy appointed time ! O give strength to bear up under Thy sweet, sweet Presence ! If Thou, O glorious, Thou the Chief of Ten Thousands, the Eternal Wonder, and Admiration of Angels and Redeemed Saints put not to me more strength, this weak clay vessel will rend in pieces under the unspeakably glorious manifestations of Thy Rich Grace and Matchless, Matchless Presence ! "

In prison, he wrote his Last and Dying Testimony. It is one of the most remarkable of Covenanter Testimonies. It is written truly by one who knew that he " had been lying dying and rotting in his blood red sins, and One had passed by and in His Love and Life said Live, Live." It is a pæan of praise and closes thus in moving harmony, " Be not afraid at His Sweet, Lovely and Desirable Cross, for although I have not been able because of my wounds to lift up or lay down my head, but as I was helped, yet I was never in better case all my life. He has not given me one challenge since I came to prison for anything less or more ; but on the contrary He has so wonderfully shined on me with the sense of His redeeming, strengthening, assisting, supporting, through bearing, pardoning and reconciling love, grace and mercy, that my soul doth long to be freed of bodily infirmities and earthly organs that so I may flee to His Royal Palace even the Heavenly Habitation of my God where I am sure of a crown put on my head, and a palm put in my hand, and a new song in my mouth, even the song of Moses and of the Lamb, that so I may bless, praise, magnify and extol Him for what He hath done to me and for me. Wherefore I bid farewell to all my dear fellowsufferers for the testimony of Jesus, who are wandering in dens and caves. Farewell my children, study holiness in all your ways, and praise the Lord for what He hath done for me, and tell all my Christian friends to praise Him on my account. Farewell sweet Bible, and wanderings and contendings for truth. Welcome death. Welcome the City of my God where I shall see Him and be enabled to serve Him eternally with full freedom. Welcome blessed company, the angels and spirits of just men made perfect. But above all, welcome, welcome, welcome, One Glorious and alone God, Father, Son and Holy Ghost, into Thy Hands I commit my soul for Thou art worthy. Amen."

His greatly-longed-for Friday came. He was taken before the Council and out from them into the thronging city streets where the crowds watched the stalwart figure of the many wounds, " eyes lifted up to Heaven, his face shining visibly."

There was a bright happiness about him from communion with God. He spoke little to the people till he came down the hill " of the sanctified bends of the Bow " into the Grassmarket, and saw his gallows-tree. Jumping up upon the scaffold he called aloud, " my soul doth magnify the Lord ! my soul doth magnify the Lord ! I have longed these sixteen years to seal the precious cause and interest of Precious Christ with my blood. And now, now He hath answered and granted my request, and has left me no more ado but to come here and pour forth my last prayers, sing forth my last praise to Him in time on this sweet and desirable scaffold, mount that ladder, and then I shall quickly get Home to my Father's House, see, enjoy, serve and sing forth the praises of my Glorious Redeemer, for evermore world without end."

He then spoke to the assembled crowds, earnestly urging them to hide in Christ from swift coming judgments, and the soldiers thundered upon their drums to drown out his voice. His choice of Scripture was the Eighth of Romans ; the choice of many another dying Covenanter. Did he read from the Manuscript New Testament ? He prayed with deep spiritual understanding in a loud clear voice, and sang the first six verses of the 34th Psalm :

> " God will I bless all times : His praise
> My mouth shall still express.
> My soul shall boast in God : the meek
> Shall hear with joyfulness.
> Extol the Lord with me ; let us
> Exalt His name together.
> I sought the Lord ; He heard, and did
> Me from all fears deliver."

And so died, aged fifty-eight, the gallant and godly John Nisbet " with the full assurance of his interest in the ever-blessed Lord Jesus Christ."

That same day, December 4th, 1685, another brave heart was stilled in Edward Marshall of Kaemuir. He too died with the glow of Salvation bright upon him—" out of love to Christ," he wrote, " and His Covenanted Work." He left a wife and seven children. Oh, the battle of the Cloister and the Hearth in the heart of a saint ! Which is to come first ? The work of God, or wife and family ? With our own, with one another, and with all concerned there is utmost need of patience and of tenderness. In Sir Walter Scott's *Journal* pages 8 and 9, Moore is quoted as having said, " more mean things have been done in the world under the shelter of wife and children than under any pretext worldlimindedness can resort to." So are we beset with peril in the most blessed place of earthly life— home. "As an angel of light," says Paul, " as an angel of light !" So may come the angel of the bottomless pit, and not be so easily recognised by the warm fireside's kindly glow, as in many another place.

But Edward Marshall won through and commended his " wife and seven children to the good guiding of my God who hath hitherto protected me : for He has promised to be a husband to the widow, and a father to the fatherless, providing they will walk in His ways, and keep His commandments. Now, I commend my soul to God, who hath preserved me hitherto and who unexpectedly has singled me out to suffer for Him, who am the unworthiest of all sinners, and I never thought that He should have so highly privileged me, as to account me worthy to give a testimony for Him, though sometimes it entered into my thoughts, ' Oh, if I should be called to it ! ' " And the call came, and having the Spirit of the Bride he was ready.

His testimony has the glorious echo in it of John Cochran, Shoemaker, who two years earlier, being hanged with two other Covenanters, and leaving a wife and six children, testified as he thought of the hardship endured, " that was no discouragement to me ; for when the storm blew hardest, the smiles of my Lord were at the sweetest. It is a matter of rejoicing unto me to think how my Lord hath passed by many a tall cedar, and hath laid His love upon a poor bramble bush the like of me."   Amen.

> " God's saints are shining lights ; who stays
> Here long must pass
> O'er dark hills, swift streams, and steep ways
> As smooth as glass,
> But these all night,
> Like candles shed
> Their beams, and light
> Us into bed."

James Renwick

" The Word of God
By Cameron thundered, or by Renwick poured
In gentle stream ; then rose the song, the loud
Acclaim of praise ; the wheeling plover ceased
Her plaint ; the solitary place was glad,
And on the distant cairns, the watcher's ear
Caught doubtfully at times the breeze borne note."

JAMES GRAHAME (*The Sabbath*).

NOT far from Greyfriars Kirkyard, one day, in a secondhand bookshop, I picked up an old calfbound volume, and on opening it, happily found that it was " a choice Collection of very valuable Prefaces, Lectures, and Sermons Preached upon the Mountains and Muirs of Scotland in the Hottest Time of the late Persecution, by that Faithful Minister and Martyr of Jesus Christ, The Reverend James Renwick." I saw that it had been owned, in 1780, by one of my own name. It cost me a shilling ! What a prize !

In the foreword, one writes of James Renwick : " he travelled with great pain and dilligence through the mosses, muirs and mountains, displaying the banner of the Gospel faithfully, in the dark cold stormy nights as well as in the day time, breaking the Bread of Life to his hearers. Often times, he had no better place of retirement to consult his Master's mind than a cold glen, cleugh, den or caves of the earth—and that for the unfeigned love he had to Christ, His Cause and persecuted people.

" He was hotly pursued and persecuted by open enemies, grievously reproached by many false lies and slanders spread against him by false brethren, backslidden professors, and such as ran into right hand extremes. Under all which he gave many convincing evidences that he esteemed the reproach of Christ greater riches than all the treasures in the world.

"The more he was afflicted the more the work of the Lord grew in his hand. The archers sorely wounded him but his bow abode in strength. The Lord made him immovable not only to believe, but to suffer patiently for His sake, and, at the last, He honoured him to seal with his blood those truths which he taught to others.

"His martyrdom was at the Grassmarket of Edinburgh, on February 17th, 1688. He was then twenty-six years old. He was lovely and pleasant in his life, and he obtained such a good report at his death as will make his memory sweet and savoury to the generations of the righteous while sun and moon endure."

It is a tenderly wise saying of a Father, "He that taketh away pity from his friend forsaketh the fear of the Lord." In this old foreword, it is as the foreword of William Penn to the Journal of George Fox, full of friendship's pity from knowledge of the truth, the voice of ungrudging love, "many sons have done excellently in their day, Dear George, but thou, thou excellest them all."

* * * *

In James Renwick culminated the fierce, great and grand battle of one hundred and fifty years for Scotland's spiritual freedom. It was the supply of the Spirit of God that brought forth man after man strong in the Lord and in the power of His might to finish stupendously in this man as living, able, and ready, as though he were the first and only in the Glorious Cause. Young, vigorous, zealous, tender, of delicate touch, and holy, he was a thrilling compelling figure carrying in him the convincing strength of the Early Reformers, winning at the last the commendation, "he was of old Knox's principles," and "stedfast, unmovable, always abounding in the work of the

Lord," as his fellow Covenanters gone before, with their faith
forward victory on him—the bright promise of the church set
free. To read what he wrote and what was written of him by
his contemporaries is to know that in him it was the Lord
God continuing to appear for His people. Even now

> " At mention of his name, a fragrance rare
> Of Lily of the Valley sweet,
> Of Rose of Sharon fair,
> Perfumes the heart."

He was born to weaver, Christ-trusting parents in the clachan
of Moniaive, among the hills of Glencairn, a child of faith,
coming when all the other children of Andrew and Elizabeth
Renwick had died. Whilst Andrew had been content that his
little ones were with Christ, Elizabeth had cried unto the Lord,
and was heard of Him for another male child. James came,
and was given back to the Giver, and his parents were glad when
they saw him at a very early age begin to pray and to read the
Scriptures. He was a child of tender conscience, and,
endowed with natural gifts, he grew in favour with folks around,
so that, after his time at the Parish School, friends got him to
Edinburgh to prepare him for the University where he kept his
faith, triumphed over temptations, and qualified for his Master
of Arts degree which he refused to accept because the Oath of
Allegiance was required from him.

The Oath of Allegiance was required from all in positions
of authority and from all who were to be so placed. It virtually
made the King a Pope. But in the Covenanter's Glorious Hope,
was no Pope, be he Pope or King ! They knew that nothing
could be given in exchange for their souls and so reigned as
kings in such knowledge. A Christ enlightened conscience to
them was of greater power than all kings and governments
whatsoever and altogether. The hard foolish heart of the Oath
was, " I acknowledge my said Sovereign only Supreme

Governor of this Kingdom over all persons and in all causes . . .
I shall never decline His Majesty's Power and Jurisdiction as I
shall answer to God." Such was part of the Divine Rights of
Kings supported by those who held a great deal of right for
themselves while it meant position and money. Charles II
" only Supreme Governor ! " Charles II ! He was as brutal
as Genghis Khan, as immoral as a Greek God, and as false as
the religion he died in when Priest Huddlestone, the
Benedictine, was brought into the death chamber and, according
to York, Charles " made his confession to him, was reconciled,
received The Blessed Sacrament, had the Extreme Unction . . .
and died unconcerned as became a good Christian." A good
Christian ! It was the false word for the false hooded Protestant
at the last. And York attested two papers saying that he had
found them in the king's strong box—papers written by the
hand of Charles, and the words occur in them, " One church
. . . and none can be that church but that which is called the
Roman Catholic Church." A good Christian ? No ! Rome
and Romance both claim him but he was no witness for Christ
Jesus.

Renwick remained in Edinburgh and saw martyrdoms
there. He told Patrick Walker, the Pedlar, that he watched the
public murder of Robert Garnock, in youth full flowered in
Christ, " esteemed by all to be a singular Christian, of deep
exercise, high attainments, great knowledge and experience in
the ways of the Lord. With him died other four of like love of
Christ, all happy by Christ's death destroying him that had the
power of death. Renwick with some friends lifted their
mutilated bodies and buried them, and took down from some
of the city gates, heads, hands and other parts of martyrs'
bodies. Also before this, he saw Cargil die with the shameful,
bloody rope round his neck, and his hands uplifted, as he had
been wont to pray. Other four died with him by every

expression saying, as wrote one of them, " Welcome cross ;
welcome gallows ; welcome Christ." That was a great day for
Renwick, for it was then that his heart was knit by Christ Jesus
into one with the wanderers. He never forgot the moving sight
of old dead Blest Cargil hanging on the gibbet, and the
head of young, scholarly and saintly Walter Smith reclining on
his breast. Writes Patrick Walker, " as he did cleave to him in
love and unity in life, so he died with his face upon his breast."

Towards the end of 1681, there was great need of the
Remnant binding up its ranks, and a drawing closer together of
all the praying and fellowship societies in the land, and James
Renwick with eager zest gave himself to work for God and His
people in these, called the United Societies. They chose four
young men to go abroad to study for their ministry and James
Renwick was one of them. He went to Gröningen and was a
pupil of the famous John á Marck who recommended that he
be ordained before Renwick was six months with him, and he
was soon back again in the land he loved. " I think," said he,
" that if the Lord could be tied to any place it is to the moors
and mosses of Scotland." And he wrote, " I think that within
a little there shall not be a moss or a mountain in the West of
Scotland which shall not be flowered with martyrs."

He was present at Darmead at the General Meeting of the
United Societies, October 3rd, 1683, and satisfied all there as to
his testimonies in Christ, and His Cause. A call was then given
to him to the ministry in the United Societies which he agreed
to accept, and he spoke to those assembled from Isaiah 40, 1-8,
and from Isaiah 26, 20. And so he became to many of them,
Mr. James Renwick, the only minister of Christ in all Scotland,
all others were hirelings who cared not for His sheep, and they
were His sheep, of this they were sure. They were the people
of His pasture and the sheep of His hand, and well knew the
voice of the Shepherd. At the time of the Darmead Assembly,

there were in the United Societies upwards of eighty societies with a very widely scattered but one-hearted non-Baal membership of seven thousand men, besides women and children. Among those he had his ministry, churchless, homeless and hunted, but loved, Oh, so loved ! by hearts that best can love, those in whom the love of God is shed abroad by the Holy Ghost. They were enemies of God who referred to him derisively as "James Renwick, Field-preacher, Rebel, Vagrant !"

Then followed his few years of wonderful work—four years each year worth seven. Preaching, teaching, organising, counselling, formulating Papers and Declarations, he was the strength in defence, the power for attack, in one of the most important spiritual battles of world history. All was headed up in young James Renwick. Like Hugh MacKail, he was none too strong in body, but even the strongest would have failed in the way he had to go. Writing to his dear friend, Sir Robert Hamilton, he says in one of his beautiful letters, " my business was never so weighty, so multiplied, and so ill to be guided to my apprehensions, as it hath been this year ; and my body was never so frail. Excessive travel, night wanderings, unseasonable sleep, and diet, and frequent preaching in all seasons of weather especially in the night, have so debilitated me that I am often incapable for any work, I fall into fits of swooning and fainting. When I use means for my recovery I find it some ways effectual ; but my desire to the work, and the necessity and importunity of the people prompts me to do more than my natural strength will allow, and to undertake such toilsome business as casts my body down again. I mention not this through any anxiety, quarrelling or discontent, but to show you my condition in this respect. I may say that under all my frailties and distempers I find great peace and sweetness in reflecting upon the occasion thereof ; it is a part of my glory and joy to bear such infirmities, contracted through my poor and small labour in my Master's Vineyard." Whoso reads the Letters of Samuel Rutherford should also read the Letters of James Renwick. There is the man, his heart, his life and love, all visible. Of these letters, J. King Hewison says, " the letters of this simple peasant, for grace, elegance of diction, and delicacy of feeling, are comparable with the best productions of his age, and afford a striking contrast to the miserable, vulgar, illspelled compositions of the fashionable hacksters who hunted the rebels to death."

In the year 1685, King James summoned a Scots Parliament, and ignorant nobles with a great deal of choler, bad taste and bad temper made acts, a bevy of them, as Satan-faced and Satan-voiced as were ever made giving his Romish Majesty armies of men between sixteen and sixty years of age, and abundance of supplies ; a mock Protestantism for Scotland, and heavy fines to be paid by the husbands of wives who would not listen to the timber-tuned preachers of it ! treason to be among the godly, and saying Yea and Amen to the Covenants of 1638 and 1643 ; sentence of death, and the taking away of everything belonging to hearers and preachers at field meetings —and a lot more besides, all having one dire aim, to exterminate for ever the " new sect sprung up among us from the dunghill, the very dregs of the people . . . whose idol is that accursed paper, the Covenant."

King Robert Bruce, a few hundred years before Covenant times, when was signed, at Arbroath, the Independence of Scotland, wrote that as long as one hundred Scotsmen were alive their country would be defended. It was a noble vow in a noble cause. In Blackgannoch Moss, in the end of May, 1685, two hundred Scotsmen gathered—two hundred Christian Scotsmen. A nobler vow they made in a Nobler Cause. They were there from their shelters in the mosses, caves, haystacks, dykesides and churchyards, and their leader was James Renwick, slim and pale with the gentleness of Christ upon him, but with no timidity of compliance. By faith that Parliament, " without the camp bearing His Reproach," had a bruised Satan under their feet.

The two hundred Covenanters at Blackgannoch " bearing in their bodies the marks of the Lord Jesus " are an interesting sight. Let a cruel and bloody king following his fathers, and a mad bloodlusting Parliament legislate murder for him, there was no fear in the faith of those Christ-thrilled souls, and they triumphed above every power that could be brought against them. They overcame their world, by faith. At Blackgannoch, they framed their Protestation and Declaration for always to be known as the " Second Declaration of Sanquhar." That little town was not very far away, and they marched to it as good, purposeful Richard Cameron, the Lion of the Covenant, and his brave hearts had done a few years before, and there again— oh, the blessed againness of the things of faith !—the Psalm, the prayer, and the determined fixing of the Declaration at the Town Cross. King, Parliament, Church and Army, all heard afresh and clear that " the bleeding remnant " would obey God rather than men, and live, and die if need be, for the Crown Rights of their Redeemer. It is quite evident that Renwick both wrote the Second Declaration of Sanquhar and proclaimed it : " Let King Jesus reign, and all His enemies be scattered."

*   *   *   *

Wrote Paul to Timothy, when about to die, " Take Mark and bring him with thee, for he is profitable to me for the ministry." It was not always so. There was a time when Paul had little use for the young man who " went not with them to the work." But there came about a blessed change, and such an one as "Paul the aged" would have with him in the Roman prison, John Mark. And old Alexander Peden, the Prophet of the Covenant, "in deaths oft," was truly dying now in his cave, and he must see the young man Renwick whom he had never met, but of whom he had believed some hard things. By all his afflictions, Puir Auld Sandie was hastening on to the joy of his Lord, and he sent for James Renwick. Patrick Walker tells the fine old story. " He said to James Wilson, that from the time he drank in these false reports, and followed these unhappy advices, it had not been with him as formerly ; and when he was adying, he sent for Mr. Renwick, who hasted to him and found him lying in very low circumstances overgrown with hair, and few to take care of him, as he never took much care of his body, and seldom unclothed himself, or went to bed. When Mr. James came in, he raised himself, upon his bed, leaning upon his elbow with his head upon his hand, and said, ' Sir, are ye the Mr. James Renwick that there is so much noise about ? ' He answered, ' Father, my name is James Renwick ; but I have given the world no ground to make any noise about me ; for I have espoused no new principle or practice, but what our Reformers and Covenanters maintained. ' Well, sir,' said Mr. Peden, ' turn about your back.' Which he did in his condescending temper. Mr. Peden said, ' I think your legs too small, and your shoulders too narrow, to take on the whole Church of Scotland on your back ; sit down, sir, and give me an account of your conversion, and of your call to the ministry, of your principles, and the grounds of your taking such singular courses, in withdrawing from all other ministers. Which Mr. Renwick did in a distinct manner ; of the Lord's way of dealing with him since infancy, and of three mornings successive in some retired place in the King's Park, where he used to frequent before he went abroad, where he got very signal manifestations and confirmations of his call to the ministry, and got the same renewed in Holland a little before he came off ; with a distinct short account of his grounds upon which he contended against tyranny and defections, and kept up an active testimony against all the evils of that day. When ended, Mr. Peden said, ' Ye have answered me to my soul's satisfaction, and I am very sorry that I should have believed any such ill reports of you, which have not only quenched my love to you, and marred my sympathy with you, but made me express myself too bitterly against you, for which I have sadly smarted. But, sir, ere you go you must pray for me, for I am old, and going to leave the world.' Which he did with more than ordinary enlargement ; when ended, he took him by the hand, and drew him to him, and kissed him and said, ' Sir, I find you a faithful servant to your Master ; go on in a single dependence upon the Lord, and ye will win honestly through and cleanly off the stage, when many others that hold their head high will fall and lie in the mire, and make foul hands and garments ' ; then prayed, that the Lord might spirit, strengthen, support and comfort him in all duties and difficulties. James Wilson was witness to this, and James Nisbet, who then lived in that countryside, could have asserted the truth of this."

They never met again. Peden, ever a phantom to the troopers, evaded them to the last, but forty days after he was buried, as he said they would, they dug him up and hung him on a gallows, and out of contempt for him, reburied him at the gallows foot. But his lowly bed became the last resting place for the folks of Cumnock Town.

> " Think ! no more in the old graveyard,
> Will anyone bury his dead !
> They carry them high to the Gallows Hill
> And lay them there at his head."

And shot Covenanters, David Dunn and Simon Paterson, lie by his side.

*   *   *   *

Renwick hastened on, Christ the fruit of his labour, and

JAMES   RENWICK

THE COMMUNION

knowing, as Peden had said, " Grace is young Glory ! "
Making full proof of his ministry, he showed himself as given
to the Lord and unto His People, by the Will of God. A
hundred escapes he had, remarkable deliverances, but the
inevitable often cast its shadow, and, one winter night in
Edinburgh, he lodged in the house of a friend, and was found
there in the early morning. He tried to escape but was badly
injured by a cruel blow which made him fall down several times
as he tried to run, and " the dog Renwick " was taken. Put in
irons, he there called upon the Lord to carry him through his
sufferings to His Praise. On being examined, with apostolic
boldness he testified calmly and clearly to his preaching of
Christ and Him Crucified. Two little note books were found in
his clothes, and in them were the heads of two sermons lately
preached—" these treasonable sermons." His indictment
makes us shake our heads with very shame as we read of the
childishness, and the barbaric heathen savagery of " the powers
that be ; ordained by God "—the stewards of God for the good
of society and yet the cursers of it. It is a short indictment
making out Renwick to be an utter villain and traitor. " You,
the said Mr. James Renwick, having shaken off all fear of God,
and respect and regard to his majesty's authority and laws ; and
having entered yourself into the society of some rebels of most
damnable and pernicious principles and disloyal practices, you
took upon you to be a preacher to those traitors and became so
desperate a villain that you did openly and frequently preach
in the fields," and so on, and so on. It is a relief to turn from
it all, to him, " the prisoner of Christ Jesus."

His father dead, a sword piercing her own soul also his
prayerful mother, when she was allowed to, came to see him.
The compassion of the Good Shepherd in him, he told her that
he was troubled at being taken away from his widely scattered
flocks but that he was trusting the Chief Shepherd to meet their

F

need, and that he was sure he had fed them wisely and led them in the right way. One time, on her asking him how he fared, he told her that he was very well, but that since his last examination by his judges, he could not get to prayer at all. On seeing her concern, he smiled and added, " I can hardly get praying, I am so taken up in praising, and am ravished with the joy of the Lord." He was reigning in Christ, reigning in the grace of God, and the Lord to him was " as the light of the morning, when the sun riseth, even a morning without clouds, as the tender grass springing out of the earth by clear shining after rain." She confessed to him, " O James, sometimes I think that I shall faint in the day of battle. How shall I look up to your head and hands set up upon the city gates ? I have so much of self I shall not be able to endure it." But he, used to looking at things unseen, assured her that this would never be. " I have willingly parted with my life," said he, " and have humbly sought of the Lord to bind them up from going any farther, and I am much persuaded they shall not be permitted to go any further." And so it was that he who when free among the hills was sometimes troubled lest he should fail his Lord when brought to judgment, was now, when bound and in prison, dwelling in a peaceable habitation, kept by the power of God. Very few of those who bore the reproach of Christ were allowed to see him. To them by his every attitude and word he said, " I press toward the mark for the prize of the high calling of God in Christ Jesus."

Early in February, 1688, the dark dawning of a bright year, he was again brought into court and his indictment again read to him. He was asked if he adhered to his former confession, and did he acknowledge all that was in his libel. Having no advocate, he counted himself happy to be permitted to speak for himself, with earnest dignity standing to all that he had formerly admitted. But he objected to the sharp part in the indictment which said that he had cast off all fear of God. "That I deny," he said, "for it is because I fear to offend God, and violate His law, that I am here standing ready to be condemned." Asked if he owned King James to be his lawful Sovereign, he answered, "No! I own all authority that has its prescriptions and limitations from the Word of God; but I cannot own this usurper as lawful king, seeing both by the Word of God such a one is incapable to bear rule, and also by the ancient laws of the kingdom which admit none to the Crown of Scotland until he swear to defend the Protestant Religion, which a man of his profession cannot do." He was then asked, "how can you deny him to be king? Is he not the late king's brother? Has the late king any children lawfully begotten? Is James not successor of Charles by Act of Parliament?" All these questions he answered very straightforwardly, saying in his summing up of James, "That from the Word of God that ought to be the rule of all laws, or from the ancient laws of the Kingdom, it could not be shown that he had, or ever could have, any right to be king."

The question as to whether Charles II had any children lawfully begotten or not was a pitiful one to ask from such a man as James Renwick. He was as pure, as fresh and as clean in his life, as Charles had been corrupt and vile. Children lawfully begotten? No! Charles II had no children lawfully begotten. The answer of James Renwick was "What children he had I do not know." But the cruel truth is out long ago. Of his children unlawfully begotten, thirteen grew up to manhood and womanhood.

Renwick was then asked if he owned and had taught that it was unlawful to pay cesses and taxes to his majesty. His answer was that it was unlawful so to do, adding, "would it have been thought lawful for the Jews in the days of Nebuchadnezzar to have brought every one a coal to augment the flame of the furnace, to devour the three children, if so they had been required by the tyrant ? And how can it be lawful, either to oppress people for not bowing to the idols the king sets up, or for their brethren to contribute what may help forward their oppression on that account ? " And so it went on, question and answer, the lone witness for Christ, no man standing by him, being carried through and over the fleshly minds of the strongly placed, salvationless men. As became the saint that he was, he told them that he would give his blood as a testimony as readily as give his word. And they having the same urge as had some of old when by wicked hands they crucified and slew the Holy and the Just, sentenced him to die. But one or two of them showed conscience ; one, Somerville, actually running away when Renwick directed some speech to them. He said that he trembled to think to take away the life of such a pious-like man though he should lose his whole estate. The young Covenanter was sentenced to die in the Grassmarket the following Friday and was asked by Linlithgow if he desired longer time. He answered, " It is all one to me. If it is protracted it is weclome. If it is shortened it is welcome. My Master's time is the best." He was then taken back to prison and his execution deferred till the 17th February. This favour was granted in the hope that he would recant, but he said that he had never asked for such leniency, and stood firm, winning the testimony that " he was of Old Knox's principles."

John Bunyan's Greatheart tells us of Mr. Fearing, " I took notice of what was very remarkable ; the water of that river was lower at this time than ever I saw it in all my life. So he went over at last, not much above wet shod." And that is lovely. James Renwick was not Mr. Fearing, but he knew that Someone would measure out the waters for him too, and his cry of faith was, " Our Jordan is before us ; it will be very deep, but it will not be very broad." He lived by the faith of the Son of God,

" Away with poverty stricken sense," he said, " which ever constructs God's Heart to be as His Face. Faith is a noble thing ; it soars high, it can read love in God's Heart when His Face frowns." The Cross of Christ was his joy, " I have found Christ's Cross sweet and lovely, I have had many joyful hours and not a fearful thought since I came hither."

Though treated kindly enough in prison, he was not allowed fellowship with any known Covenanter. Others came of varied theological and religious colours whose hues pleased a King and State who were actually colour blind as far as religion was concerned. They all felt the false thrill of being on the side of power and pitied the young man who interpreted the Holy Scriptures into principles he was losing his life for. Thumbscrew Bishop Paterson came asking, " Do you think that none can be saved but those of your principles ? Will you kill yourself with your own hand, seeing that you can have your life upon easy terms ?" But when the heart is given the word is readily found in the mouth, and it was with no uncertainty in the worthwhileness of his devotion that Renwick made answer, " I never said or thought none could be saved but such as were of my principles, but I am of the opinion that those truths for which I suffer are sufficient grounds to suffer upon."

In gown and canonical habit, one named MacNaught got entrance to him, and Renwick told him that he did not like his coat, it was a bad badge. But he conversed with him. Frequently, priests of Rome came and with every visit left more and more convinced that the young Covenanter was certainly a hell-going heretic. And the jailors had a saying among them, " Begone, as Renwick said to the priests ! " And so it was that though his Word-of-Life hearers in the shadowed glens would listen to him no more, his mission continued to the last amongst those whose zeal made them persecute the Church of God. To them it was given to see a young man count all things but loss for the excellency of the knowledge of Christ Jesus his Lord.

Three days before he was hanged, he was again brought before the Council and there witnessed cheerfully that he was glad that he was counted worthy to suffer shame for Christ. He told a friend who kindly asked how he was, that he was very well but that he expected to be much better in a few days. To his mother he said that he saw need for his suffering at this time, believing that his death would do far more good than his life would have done were he to live many years.

Writing was denied to him while in the condemned cell, even as friends were. He had begun to write a testimony but pen, ink and paper had been taken from him. Yet how it was, it is not known, the night before his execution he had a testimony written, and got it out. It is fully given in the grand old book, " The Cloud of Witnesses," where it can be read and re-read with spiritual profit. It carries the power of the Covenanter, that of the Cross. It begins on earth and finishes in Heaven. Here is the latter part of it, to his loved fellows. " He has strengthened me to brave man and face death, and I am now longing for the joyful hour of my dissolution, and there is nothing in the world that I am sorry to leave but you ; but I go to better company, and so I must take my leave of you all. Farewell beloved sufferers, and followers of the Lamb ; farewell Christian intimates ; farewell Christian and comfortable Mother and Sisters ; farewell sweet societies ; farewell desirable general meetings ; farewell night wanderings in cold and weariness for Christ ; farewell sweet Bible and preaching of the Gospel ; farewell sun, moon and stars, and all sublunary things; farewell conflicts with a body of sin and death. Welcome scaffold for Precious Christ ; welcome heavenly Jerusalem ; welcome innumerable company of angels ; welcome general assembly and church of the first born ; welcome crown of glory, white robes and songs of Moses and the Lamb, and, above all, Welcome, O Thou blessed Trinity and one God ! O eternal One ! I commit my soul into Thy eternal rest."

He wrote also " A Letter to His Christian Friends." It speaks of loyalty to God and to his fellow Covenanters. Here are short parts of it. " Yesterday I was cast into a deep exercise, and made to dwell under an impression of the dreadfulness of everything that might grieve the Spirit of God. I found sin to be more bitter than death, and one hour's hiding of God's face more insupportable . . . They also urged me, upon pain of torture to tell where out societies were, who kept our general correspondences ; and where were they kept ? I answered, though they should torture me, which was contrary to all law, after sentence of death, I would give them no further notice than the books gave." His two little books ! " I was, moreover, threatened to tell my haunts and quarters, but I refused to make known to them any such thing ; so I was returned to prison. Such exercises as I had were very needful to me for such a trial ; and I would rather endure what they could do unto me, than have dishonoured Christ, offended you, and brought you into trouble. But I hope, within less than three days, to be without the reach of all temptations. Now I have no more to say :—Farewell again in our Blessed Lord Jesus."

* * * *

On February 17th, 1688, out of the cold darkness of a wintry night, the light of day struggled, to lie a grey leaden sea above the hills and valleys of Edinburgh. The waking thought of thousands that chill morning was of James Renwick that day in faith to die, not yet receiving the promise of the Church of Christ set free. By the end of the year, there would be freedom and light, but the day of his testimony and death was a day of chains and darkness, and he in the grim blackness of it all fearing no evil.

Helpers in sorrow, and the sorrow-laden are early astir, and James Renwick's mother and young sisters were soon on their anxious way to the prison house to eat a little with him, and to worship. There is an incomparable fellowship of His Presence in the breaking of bread. There everything and every act are all of one if we will have it so, symbolising the greatest act of all, the Act of God, Christ broken for us. When the young Covenenter returned thanks that morning, he said, " O Lord, Thou hast brought me within two hours of eternity, and this is no matter of terror to me, more than if I were to lie down in a bed of roses ; nay, through grace, to Thy praise, I may say I never had the fear of death, since I came to this prison ; but from the place where I was taken, I could have gone very composedly to the scaffold. O ! how can I contain this, to be within two hours of the crown of glory."

Responsibility and experience take from us fancied knowledge, and in place of it reveal reality. So James Renwick with a trial of faith more precious than of perishing gold was well fitted to speak to his loved ones on life and death. He said to them, " Death is the king of terrors but not to me now, as it was some times in my hidings ; but now let us be glad and rejoice for the marriage of the Lord is come, and His wife hath made herself ready. Would ever I have thought that the fear of suffering and of death could be so taken from me ? What shall I say to it ? It is the doing of the Lord and marvellous in our eyes. I have many times counted the cost of following Christ but never thought it would be so easy, and now who knows the honour and happiness of that, ' He that confesses me before men, him will I confess before the Father.' " His mother wept and with disciplined tenderness he said to her, "Remember, Mother, they who love anyone better than they do Christ Jesus, are not worthy of Him. Rejoice with me that I am going to my Father to obtain the enjoyment of what eye hath not seen, nor ear heard, neither hath entered into the heart of man the things that God hath prepared for them that love Him !"

God so loved us that He gave His only Begotten Son for us upon the Cross. The Son of God so loved us that He left the Presence of His Father to agonise in the lonely darkness of the Cross, crying, " My God, my God, why hast Thou forsaken me ?" Such is the love of the Father and of the Son for humanity. So James Renwick was following in the steps of the Example given. His hating himself and his loved ones, his forsaking all, and his taking up of the cross, were all born out of the love of God—the hate that draws its life from love.

He went to prayer that lifted into loving praise, to heart-breaking, loving intercession for the afflicted of the Lord, His Own, and then up again into praise, the heart filled with the everlasting Song, " Worthy is the Lamb that was slain." The drums thundered for the guard, and officials nervously made for their posts. The crowds began to surge along the narrow streets, the godly praying and the loving weeping. The martyr smiled. They were his drums now, not theirs. All things were his. In triumphant joy, he shouted, " Yonder is the welcome warning to my marriage ; the Bridegroom is coming ; I am ready, I am ready."

Love is ever on the Cross or standing near it, albeit weeping. If it lapses, it may follow afar off and broken-heartedly repent. But it never sits down and coldly watches Him there. And so it was as the last leader of the Wanderers, and his loved ones, broke apart from one another for the last time, the cross was taken by them all and held fast by love, and he turned towards the gallows by way of the Low Council House, where he was asked to say what he had to say, and to pray what he had to pray, for when he should get to the scaffold no word would be permitted him either to man or to God. The drums would drum, and drum, and drum again, until the only sound in all the world would be the sound of drums, and the only sight his death. The Covenanter answered that he had

prepared nothing either to pray or to say, but that the Holy
Spirit would be His Guide. It is the answer of the prepared
spirit. They asked him if he would like one of their ministers
to be with him. He said, " No ! If I would have had any of
them for my counsellors or comforters, I should not have been
here this day. I require none with me but this one man," his
friend who waited on him. So set off the melancholy procession,
but he with a happy cheerfulness on him.

By the side of the scaffold, a curate said, " Own our king
and we shall pray for you." He answered, " I will have none
of your prayers ; I am come to bear my testimony against you,
and such as you are." The curate persisted, " own our king
and pray for him, whatever you say against us." And Renwick
replied, " I will discourse no more with you ; I am within a
little to appear before Him who is King of kings, and Lord of
lords, who shall pour shame, contempt and confusion upon all
the kings of the earth who have not ruled for Him." Calvary,
besides being everything else that matters, was an affair of
kings too, earthly, heavenly, over man and in him, and was the
Victory of the King. How blessed to die in the grace and power
of it as died James Renwick.

While the drums beat out their wild disharmony he
magnified and blessed the Lord in singing from the 103rd Psalm,
and in reading his last chapter, Revelation 19. Amid all the
din, his manly voice thrilled with rapturous faith as he read the
words. " He hath on His vesture and on His thigh a name
written King of Kings and Lord of Lords." To prayer he
went again while the drums continued their deafening earthborn,
earthbound thunder, and was heard of Him in Heaven, His
Dwelling Place.

Humanly, he complained about being disturbed in worship,
but assured himself afresh, " I shall soon be above these clouds ;
then shall I enjoy Thee and glorify Thee without interruption

or intermission forever." The harsh order was given to him to go up the death ladder. He climbed up and prayed again, being heard to say, " Lord, I die in the faith that Thou wilt not leave Scotland, but that Thou wilt make the blood of Thy witnesses the seed of Thy church, and return again and be glorious in our land. And now, Lord, I am ready ; The Bride, the Lamb's wife, hath made herself ready." The blinding napkin was tied about his face, and he spoke to his friend, close by his side, " Farewell ; be diligent in duty, make your peace with God through Christ. There is a great trial coming. As to the remnant I leave, I have committed them to God. Tell them from me not to weary nor be discouraged in maintaining the testimony, and the Lord will provide you teachers and ministers ; and when He comes, He will make these despised truths glorious in the earth," and with his last words in his mouth, " Lord, into Thy hands I commend my spirit, for Thou has redeemed me, Lord God of Truth," the hangman turned him over. The testimony to Christ defying drums never ceased their cruel rattling until the death struggles of one of the sweetest martyrs of Jesus were ended. So died the last leader, the beautiful and saintly last leader of the Covenanters, three days beyond his twenty-sixth birthday, joining as he said, " my testimony to all that hath been sealed by blood, shed either on scaffolds, fields or seas for the Cause of Christ." He died for the Crown Rights of the Redeemer against the infamous, impious usurpation of the Stuart kings, of what he, inspired-like, had called "The Uncommunicable Prerogative of Jehovah," the Headship of the Kirk of the Living God. Helen Alexander, a sufferer in the same cause, reverently wrapped him in his winding sheet, and he was laid away, among the dust of other martyrs in the most despised and neglected corner of Greyfriars Kirkyard, the burial place of criminals, a " grave with the wicked."

*　　*　　*　　*

The leaderless, Bleeding Remnant, through the dark months, struggled on living and dying, in their "sweet believing," their very enduring their achieving. The last of them known to fall before the Glorious Revolution was George Wood, of Andrew Hislop's age, sixteen or seventeen years, and, like that brave, godly shepherd boy, he lay in the fields. The lines written so feelingly by Dr. Veitch of Andrew Hislop will also ever speak of young, fellow-martyr George Wood shot in the night, the night indeed just before the dawn.

> " So they left you, martyr brave,
>   Left you on the reddened sod ;
>   But no raven touched your face ;
>   On it lay the peace of God."

Epilogue

What were their losses, and what their gains? Their losses were themselves and all that they had. Their gains were great, not for themselves but for posterity. They, with their fellows, the Puritans, gained freedom in every realm of human living, thus winning and preserving democracy, and the right to spiritually and morally worship God with an open Bible interpreted by all. They were the pioneers of the Protestant intellectual renaissance, resulting in the discovery of so much for the good of man in his earth environment, accompanied by laws for the community in social ameliorations whose good can never be calculated. All byproducts of the Gospel had to have a preserved Gospel. They were the preservers. They made possible the lawfulness of dissent in times of error, coldness and ecclesiastical death; cleared the way and dug the foundations of every religious revival we have since known, and were the first in the missionary enterprise. To them we owe our way of life, our constitution, our institutions, our commonwealth, and our honoured place among the nations of the world. But for them our place, and that of the U.S.A., would have been low down among the Romanist nations with the grimly attendant dire consequences of such a plight, the menace of atheistic Communism.

Their faith held no lifeless opinions. It was as spiritual and evangelical as they themselves were, alive unto God, taken up with the Person of the Lord Jesus Christ. So dear is their memory, so sure their testimony, that for us it must be, " Whose faith follow, considering the end of their manner of life, Jesus Christ the same yesterday, and to-day, and forever."

Bibliography

Six Saints of the Covenant	....	2 Vols.	Patrick Walker.
The Covenanters	....	2 Vols.	Dr. J. King Hewison.
Men of the Covenant	....	....	Dr. Alex. Smellie.
Memoirs of James Frazer			
Naphtali	....	Sir James Stewart.	
The Scots Worthies	....	....	John Howie.
The Cloud of Witnesses	....	....	Dr. J. H. Thomson.
Ladies of the Covenant	....	....	James Anderson.
The Harp of the Covenant		....	John MacFarlane.
The Treasury of the Covenant	....	J. C. Johnston.	
Letters of Samuel Rutherford			
Letters of James Renwick			
The Christian's Great Interest	....	William Guthrie.	
The Makers of the Kirk	....	....	T. Ratcliffe Barnett.

Jamieson & Munro, Ltd., Printers, Stirling.